Published in 2011 by Stewart, Tabori & Chang
An imprint of ABRAMS.

Library of Congress Cataloging-in-Publication Data:
Occhipinti, Lisa.
 The repurposed library / Lisa Occhipinti.
     p. cm.
 ISBN 978-1-58479-909-2 (alk. paper)
1. Altered books. I. Title.
 TT896.3.O255 2010
 745.5--dc22
                              2010020797

Editor: Liana Allday
Designer: Meg Mateo Ilasco
Production Manager: Tina Cameron

The text of this book was composed in Proxima Nova, Trade Gothic, and Brownstone Sans.

Printed and bound in Hong Kong, China
10 9 8 7 6 5 4 3 2 1

THE ART OF BOOKS SINCE 1949

115 West 18th Street
New York, NY 10011
www.abramsbooks.com

For Evelyn Grace

CONTENTS

Introduction

As a child I adored books, despite the fact that I hated to read. What I loved was the object of the book, its feel in my hands, the whisper of flipping pages, and of course, illustrations. My mother kept a family Bible in her nightstand that I would quietly seek out from time to time. I wouldn't read a word, but I would marvel at the translucent, onionskin pages and the faux shagreen cover embossed with gilt letters.

Since childhood, my passion for books has only grown. Around age ten I realized that I enjoyed reading books—not just looking at them. In junior high school I started to write thoughts and poetry and to sketch on the pages of blank journals. And in college I began to see books as a form I could create entirely from scratch, choosing not just the content but the size, the paper, and the covers. My first one featured a collection of photos I had taken based on the five senses, and was bound together using a simple side-sewn Japanese technique. I loved how I was able to arrange my images into a cohesive, interactive form.

After college, my appetite whetted, I took courses to learn more about creating books. With these new skills, I made blank journals and custom books with cloth-covered cases as well as leather-bound books with signatures. But then, as I am prone to do, I began to wonder what else a book could be. How could it have a greater presence? How could a book become an active object? That is when I discovered altered books—the art of giving books a new form.

I began painting and cutting the pages of books and gluing objects to their covers. I started to wonder, what if I just used the covers? What if I simply thought of the pages as paper? What if I broke down the elements of the book and used them as basic materials? I considered all of these questions in depth and began to see books in a brand-new light. What appears in *The Repurposed Library* are the results of my experiments. Many of the projects show you how to transform existing books into new art objects, such as mobiles (page 18) and wall sculptures (page 126). Other projects transform books into practical everyday objects, such as shelves (page 47), frames (page 114), and even a lamp and lampshade (pages 106 and 111).

Some projects in this book also show you how to appreciate and enhance your own library with personalized bookplates (page 60), bookmarks made from repurposed book spines (page 64), rubber-stamped book "tattoos" (page 58), and custom-made dust jackets (page 62). Detailed how-to instructions and illustrations walk you through each step of the process, from deconstructing a book to making it into something new.

I know it may seem strange for a person who loves books so much to have made a career out of deconstructing them. But repurposing a book is simply a different way of experiencing it and embracing its beauty. I feel a deep connection to the weight of a book, the tooth of its paper, and the smell of its ink (or mustiness). I wonder where books have been, who has owned them, and in what sorts of rooms they have resided. Have they been taken on vacation, and if so, where did they go? Have they been lent to friends, and were they eventually returned to their owner?

Over the last twenty years I have been building my library, voraciously collecting grand tomes and antiquated novels that speak to me. Some books are to read, some are to use in my art projects, and some are just to look at and enjoy. The sad fact is that not everyone can maintain a large library—not even public libraries—and consequently, many books get thrown out. Bookstores "remainder" titles that don't sell quickly enough, unloading them at a fraction of their original price. Libraries dispose of books with cracked spines or obsolete information, and neighbors sell off unwanted, dusty volumes for mere coins at yard sales. And with so much information available online or in electronic formats in our technology-driven world, there is a sense that physical books could become relics.

So what to do with all these orphaned books? *The Repurposed Library* is my attempt to answer that question. Whether you are transforming a book for the first time or you've been doing this your whole life, I hope that you enjoy giving new function to the books you love. You won't look at them the same way again.

CHAPTER ONE
BOOKS, TOOLS & TECHNIQUES

Every project in this book is made from books, so before you get started, there are a few things you'll need to know: Which books are best to use? Which ones are valuable and shouldn't be deconstructed? How can you repurpose a book that's falling apart? What are the various parts of a book, and what's the best way to deconstruct it for a project? The information in this chapter addresses these questions and will guide you toward making successful projects out of books.

UNDERSTANDING THE VALUE OF BOOKS

The best books to use in craft projects are ones that do not have any significant value. What is "significant value," you ask? Now, I'd be the first to say that every book has significant value, but in this case, we mean the monetary and historical worth. Valuable books are usually first-edition printings or they are rare and collectible, though it can sometimes be tricky to figure out if a book falls into either category. Following are a few guidelines to help you identify a potentially "valuable" book before you put it under the knife.

First-Edition Books

First editions are copies from the first print run of a title and are typically given more value than subsequent editions (especially if it turns out to be an important book, like a Pulitzer prize-winner). It is not always easy to identify a first edition, but the first place to look is the copyright page. In a perfect world, you'd see the words "first edition," "first printing," or "first impression" printed on the page. To indicate first editions, some publishers put their logo or colophon on this page, along with a "1" or "A" below it. And in more contemporary publishing (1950 and later), a first printing is indicated on the copyright page with a series of numbers, starting with 10 and counting down to 1. For the second printing, the 1 is removed so the 2 is the lowest number shown (and so forth for subsequent editions).

Publishers of pre-1950 books may denote a first edition in a less transparent way. If you see nothing that indicates the book's edition, you can likely find the answer by inquiring at a local rare book dealer, used bookstore, or with a librarian.

Rare and Collectible Books

Books that fall into the "rare and collectible" category include some first editions, historically significant works, literary tomes, and livres d'artistes (illustrated artists' books where each page is an original art print).

Spotting rare and collectible books is an art form in and of itself, replete with loopholes and expert-only savvy, but there are some easy ways that you can investigate a book's value. A good way to start is by talking to a local librarian or looking up the book on bookfinder.com, which is a valuable source of information.

The condition of a rare book is the most important factor in its worth. Books with a split spine or foxing (brown age spots on their pages) are less valuable. Conditions are rated as "very fine/mint" to "fair" to "reading copy," and can be tough to determine if you have little or no experience. If you are uncertain about the condition of your book, talk to a rare book dealer.

Whether or not you repurpose a rare or collectible book is a personal choice. For instance, I found a tiny copy of *A Window in Thrums* by J. M. Barrie (the author of *Peter Pan*) for a mere three dollars. The title is embossed on the red cloth cover in an elegant uppercase font, surrounded by a silver-leaf border. The copyright page simply includes a print date and publisher: 1894, Henry Altemus, Philadelphia. I looked it up on bookfinder.com, located the exact listing, and found it to have a retail value of $8.70. While this is not a mortgage payment by any means, I just couldn't bring myself to repurpose this book, finding that I appreciated it far more intact than reused for a project.

Sentimental Value

This is probably the easiest value to determine as it only involves asking yourself or someone else if the book has sentimental significance before you cut it up. If you have your eye on a book from someone else's long-neglected collection, be sure to check with the book's owner before you start working—even if you suspect that the book hasn't been opened in decades. A volume found in your mother's attic may seem like it wouldn't be missed, but it could have great sentimental value for her.

WHICH BOOKS ARE BEST TO REPURPOSE?

Look for books that meet the needs of your craft project and speak to your creative sensibilities. Consider the book's size and thickness, the cover's color, imagery or pattern, the typography and illustrations within, and of course, the subject and title itself. All of the projects included here use hardcover books—their hard outer cases are great raw material for myriad crafting projects, but hardcover books also tend to be made with higher-quality materials. Paperback books can be used, however, for projects that only use the book's pages (such as the Narrative Vases on page 131 or the Book Bursts on page 80). Since I often only need a part of a book for a project—such as the pages or just the cover—damaged books can be a great choice. So if you find a book with a lovely and viable cover that encases moldy and unusable pages, simply toss the pages in the recycling bin and use the cover by itself.

Additionally, look for books that have supple, non-brittle pages and a sturdy cover (though worn, cracked spines can be repaired; see page 14). Old, brittle pages will tear when folded, bent, glued, or otherwise manipulated. Avoid moldy, mildewed, or musty-smelling books as these can be toxic. For pointers on great places to find books, check the Resources section on page 142.

THE TOOLBOX

Here is the basic set of tools to have on hand when creating the projects in this book. Most of these tools can be obtained at a craft supply store. Specific tools for each project are listed at the beginning of the projects' instructions.

Scissors

Craft knife and extra blades (I use X-Acto #11)

Cutting mat

Pencil

Metal ruler

Self-adhesive linen bookbinding tape (used to repair a damaged book spine)

Bone folder (a flat, smooth bookbinding tool used for creasing, smoothing out paper after it has been glued and for pushing paper into small crevices)

Awl (for making small holes in paper and covers)

White glue (such as Elmer's) and glue brush (½" and/or 1" flat bristle brush)

Gluestick (in a tube)

Superglue

Glue gun and glue sticks

Newspaper (for covering your work surface when gluing)

Small office clips (also called binder or butterfly clips)

Large spring clamps (available at hardware stores)

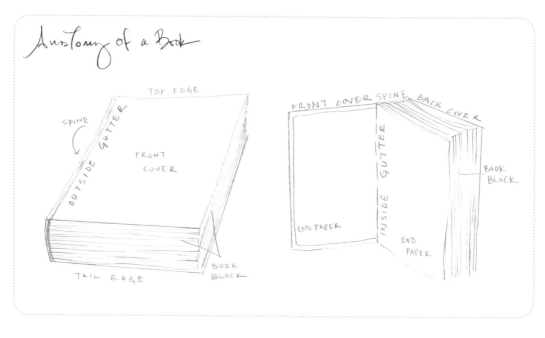

THE ANATOMY OF A BOOK

For most of the projects in this book, you'll need to deconstruct the book in one way or another to use its pieces. Before you learn how to do this, it's important to understand the anatomy of a book and the names given to its many parts.

Cover (or Case): the outer, protective casing of a book. For hardcover books, the case is usually made from boards, which are then covered in cloth, heavyweight coated paper stock, or even leather. For paperback books, the cover is usually a piece of heavyweight, coated paper stock.

Spine: The side of the book where the pages are bound together. The book's cover wraps around the spine and can be sewn in place (common for hard-cover books) or glued in place (common for paperback books), or both.

Endpapers: Two folded sheets of paper—typically of a heavier weight than the main book pages—that are pasted onto the inside front and back cover of a hardback book. One half of the endpaper is glued to the inside cover, while the other half of the sheet is left

loose, becoming the first or last "page" of the book. (The page that follows the loose endpaper is actually considered the first true page of the book.) Paperback books do not have endpapers.

Book block: All of a book's pages bound together.

Signature: A section of 8 pages printed front and back and stitched together. Sometimes you'll find a section with 4 pages printed front and back, which is called a "half-signature."

Gutter: On the inside of the book, this is the space where the pages meet when the book is opened. On the exterior of the book, the gutter is the ditch that runs along the length of the book right next to the spine (where the book hinges open).

BASIC TECHNIQUES

All the projects include step-by-step instructions, though there are a few basic techniques that are used many times throughout the book. You'll find instructions for these basic techniques in this section.

Deconstructing a Hardcover Book

In many projects you will need to "deconstruct the book," which means you'll need to take it apart. To do this, begin by removing the book block from its cover:

1. Open up the front cover and run your craft knife along the inside gutter of the book, cutting through the endpaper (see diagram below).

2. Flip to the back inside cover of the book and repeat Step 1.

3. Remove the book block from the cover.

Deconstructing a Book Block

A book block is typically composed of signatures that are glued or sewn together along one edge. If you need to use only one or two signatures from the book block, simply run your craft knife between two signatures along the outside edge of the book block's spine—each signature creates a ridge along the spine (see diagram below).

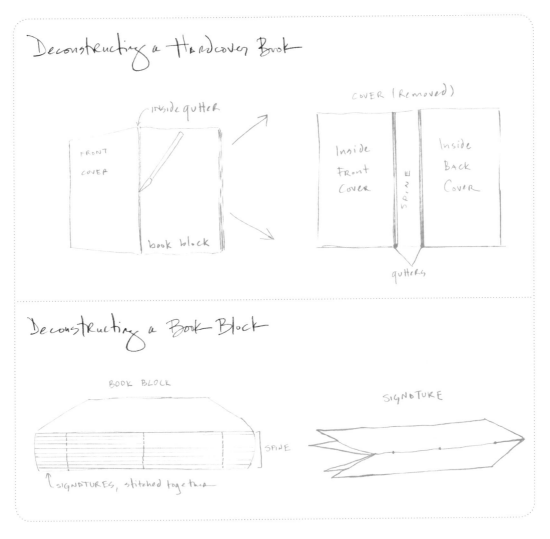

13

Repairing a Spine

If you want to work with a hardcover book but the spine is in less than ideal condition, reinforce it with linen bookbinding tape. Simply cut a length of tape long enough to cover the damaged area, wet the adhesive side (I dip my fingers lightly in water and run them along the tape), and place the tape over the damaged area on the inside of the book. Using the edge and point of a bone folder, smooth the tape into place and into any crevices along the spine (see diagram below).

Gluing

A lot of gluing is required for the projects in this book, but the most common method is gluing one paper fiber to another with white glue. The same technique is used whether you're gluing an endpaper to the inside cover of a book or a sheet of loose paper to a piece of cardboard. It's vital to know how to glue correctly, since this step will ultimately determine the longevity of the piece and stabilize your creation, ensuring that the pieces fully fuse together and, when dry, lie flat without buckling or blistering.

To glue paper and paperboards together, begin by pouring a small puddle of white glue onto scrap paper or into a small cup (rather than drizzling it directly onto the surface). Always apply glue with a glue brush, brushing it on sparingly from the center of the paper surface out to all edges (see diagram below). Lay the glued paper, glue side down, on its designated surface. Press down on it with your fingers, then smooth out the paper with the long side of a bone folder from the center outward, pushing out any air pockets or excess glue (see diagram below).

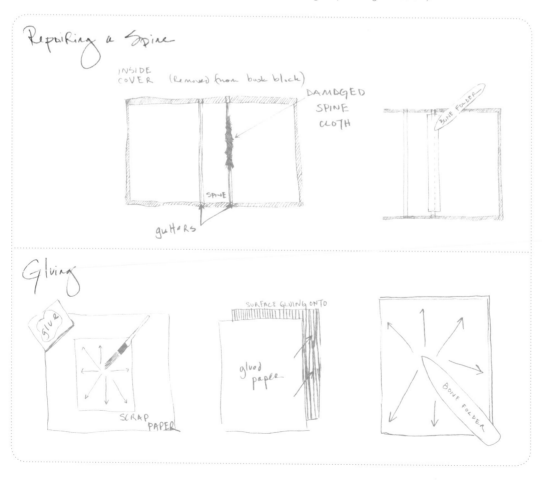

Re-Covering the Inside of a Book Cover

For many projects in this book, you will want to re-cover the original endpapers. Sometimes endpapers are damaged or are simply not all that attractive. And in projects where you have removed the book block and are working with just the case, the interior raw spine will be exposed and should be re-covered. You can use virtually any type of paper to re-cover the inside of a book, though you might want to choose papers that work with your project theme. Some of my favorite choices are pages from the interior of the book, decorative papers, art papers, or wallpaper. The only papers to avoid would be thin or brittle ones, such as tissue paper or transparent vellum.

To re-cover the inside of a book's spine:

With the inside of the book cover facing up, measure the height and width of the spine, then add 1" to the width measurement. Make sure that the new paper's grain runs in the proper direction (see right), then cut a piece of the paper to these dimensions and brush glue on the backside of the paper. Center the paper over the spine and smooth it into place with a bone folder, pushing the paper into the crevices of the gutter.

To re-cover a book's endpapers:

Measure the height and width of the existing end-papers, then subtract ¼" from the width. Make sure that the new paper's grain is running in the proper direction (see right), then cut two pieces to these di-mensions and brush glue on the backside of the paper. Adhere to the front and back interior of the book and smooth into place with a bone folder. Close the book and place a few books (or other flat, heavy objects) on top to apply pressure. Allow the glue to dry thoroughly.

Paper Grain

Though you can't see it with the naked eye, most high-quality papers—such as art paper, decorative paper, wallpaper, and even the boards used for hardcover books—have a "grain," meaning that the fibers run in one direction. When gluing and assembling paper for projects, it is important that all the grains be parallel (otherwise your project will warp). For instance, when you are re-covering the endpapers on the inside of a book cover, make sure that the paper's grain is vertical (book cover grains always run vertically).

To determine the direction of your paper's grain, simply hold the ends of the paper and bow it. If you feel tightness or resistance, you are bending it against the grain. If the paper bows easily, you are bending it along the grain. You will also find that paper tears and folds more easily along the grain. If a paper bends eas-ily both ways, then it's fine to use in any direction.

CHAPTER TWO

Projects

BOOKMOBILE

When I was growing up in New England, the Bookmobile—an orange bus that was a library on wheels—would come to my neighborhood every other Thursday in the summertime. I admit that on some days it was the air conditioning that lured me inside, but I always loved seeing all those book spines along its walls, whether it was hot outside or not.

My Bookmobile is obviously a play on words—a mobile is a free-hanging sculpture, and since mine is made from a book, it is quite literally a bookmobile. This suspended sculpture launches books into flight—which is the way books made me feel when I discovered them as a kid.

Materials

Hardcover book

Lightweight cardboard

Decorative paper, for inside cover

Tools

Craft knife

White glue and glue brush

Pencil

Metal ruler

Scissors

Bone folder

Glue gun and glue sticks

Large office clamp

Awl

Heavy-duty upholstery thread and
  sewing needle

1. Remove Book Block

Using a craft knife and following the instructions on page 13, remove the book block and set aside. Repair the book's spine, if necessary, following the instructions on page 14.

2. Reinforce Spine and Re-Cover Endpapers

Cut a piece of lightweight cardboard the same size as the book's spine. Brush glue onto the back of the cardboard and press into the spine. Then re-cover the endpapers using paper of your choice and following the instructions on page 15.

3. Select Single Pages

Go through the pages in the book block and gently cut or tear out approximately 24 pages for the decorative loops. Pages that work especially well are those with an illustration or an inscription, or a title page. Set them aside.

Plug in the glue gun so that it will be ready to use in Step 5.

4. Remove a Signature from Book Block

With a craft knife, remove one signature from the book block (see page 13); this will form the base of your sculpture.

5. Create Mobile's Base

To create the base of the mobile, gently bend the first page of the signature so that it curls in toward the gutter (Figure A). Run a thin line of hot glue along the gutter and press the page into place. Note: the glue will dry quickly so you need to work fast. Take care not to burn your fingers.

Repeat this step with the next page, working consecutively until all the pages in the signature have been bent and glued in place.

6. Create Loops

To create the decorative loops, gently bend and glue the 24 single-gle pages from Step 3 using the technique from Step 5 (Figure B).

7. Add Loops to Base

Run hot glue along the edge of a single loop and quickly insert it into a crevice between loops in the base (Figure C). Continue to insert loops into the base this way, making design decisions as you progress. Consider how wide or long you want the finished mobile form to be. Do you want a flourish of pages to be longer on one side? Will your form have an organic or symmetrical shape

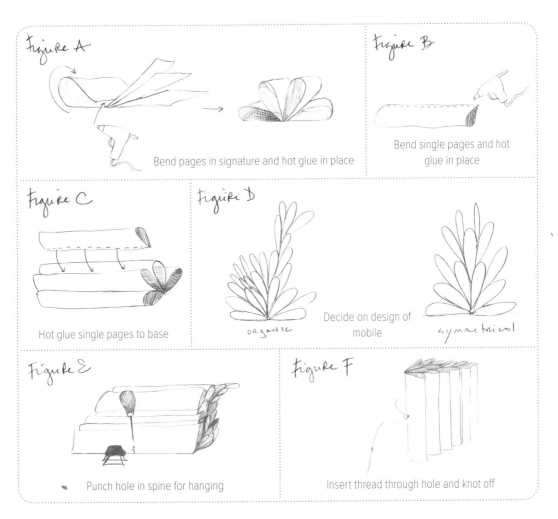

Figure A — Bend pages in signature and hot glue in place

Figure B — Bend single pages and hot glue in place

Figure C — Hot glue single pages to base

Figure D — Decide on design of mobile

organic

symmetrical

Figure E — Punch hole in spine for hanging

Figure F — Insert thread through hole and knot off

(Figure D)? As you construct the mobile, occasionally pick it up and hold it so that you can see what it will look like hanging (remember that you are essentially constructing it upside down).

8. Attach Cover to Mobile Form

Once you are pleased with the size and shape of your mobile form, clamp the spine edge of the base to keep it stable. With a pencil, measure and mark the center of the mobile form's "spine," about ½" from the edge. Punch a hole at the marked point with an awl, being sure to punch through all layers of paper (Figure E).

Next, measure and mark the center of the spine on the inside of the book cover. Make a small hole through the book cover at this point with an awl.

Thread the needle with approximately 1½ yards of thread, doubled and knotted. With the mobile form on its side, insert the needle into the hole and pull it through to the knot. Loop the needle through the hole three more times and then knot off again, but do not cut the thread (Figure F).

Align the book cover with the mobile form and draw the needle through the hole in its spine to the outside of the book cover. Pull on the thread to snugly fit the sculpted pages into the cover and tie a knot. Decide how far from the ground you want your sculpture to hang and leave enough thread to do so, making a 2" loop for hanging at the end of the thread. Lift the cover and secure the spine of the mobile form to the inside book cover with hot glue in a few places.

SEWING BOX

This clever storage box is an ideal way for sewers to stash away all their little tools. Special compartments keep needles, spools, bobbins, seam rippers, and measuring tapes organized, and a built-in pincushion adds a plush touch. A book on the subject of sewing is ideal for this project, but any book will do. This box can be used to stash other crafting and stationery tools, as well—think about the tools you use regularly and customize the compartments to suit your needs.

Materials

Hardcover book (ring binder optional)
  Note: If you would like to store spools of thread, you'll need a book at least 2" thick. A ring binder helps create extra compartments but is not necessary to complete the project.

12" x 12" sheet of decorative paper, to line the inside cover (optional)

4' length of 2"-6" wide, ⅛"-thick balsa wood

Acrylic paint (to coordinate with book)

An old sewing pattern, to line the compartments

⅛ yard cotton fabric (to coordinate with book)

Fiberfill

Tools

Craft knife

Cutting mat

White glue and glue brush

Pencil

Metal ruler

Glue gun and glue sticks

Toothpicks

Awl (for books with ring binder only)

Thin yarn and upholstery needle (for books with ring binder only)

Small, flat paintbrush with a ¼" tip

Scissors

Thread in coordinating color and sewing needle

1. Remove Book Block

Using a craft knife and following the instructions on page 13, remove the book block and set aside.

2. Cover Inside of Book (Optional)

I chose not to re-cover the endpapers of the book shown here, as they featured a great photo. If you like, re-cover your endpapers following the instructions on page 15.

3. Measure and Mark Compartments

On the inside back cover of the book, use a ruler and pencil to measure and mark ⅛" from all four edges. This rectangle will be the outer perimeter of the storage box.

Divide the height of the box into thirds and mark these measurements with pencil. Then divide the upper row and lower rows into thirds, again marking these with pencil (Figure A).

To determine the depth of the "walls," measure the width of the book's spine and subtract ⅛".

4. Create Outer Box

With the craft knife and ruler, cut four strips of balsa: two strips measuring the height of the book by the depth of the "walls"; two strips measuring the width of the book by the depth of the "wall". (Note: If your book has binder rings, extend the width of the walls past the rings to the inside of the spine, so that the rings are also encased within the balsa walls; see photo on page 23.)

Beginning with the left side wall (the one closest to and parallel to the spine), run hot glue along the bottom edge of the balsa strip and press along the pencil line. Hold in place while the glue sets.

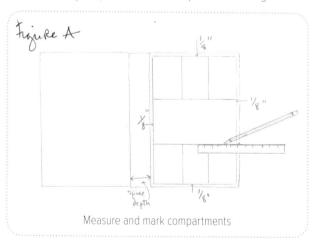

Measure and mark compartments

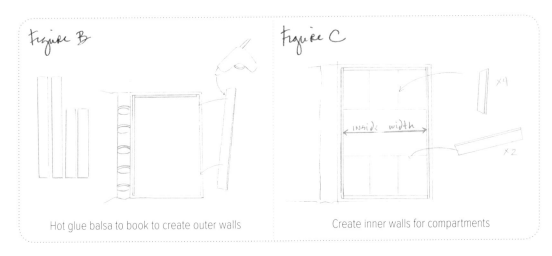

Figure B

Figure C

inside width

x4

x2

Hot glue balsa to book to create outer walls

Create inner walls for compartments

Glue the other outer walls the same way (Figure B). If the wood fits together too snugly, trim the balsa to fit. To strengthen the corners, add a drop of hot glue and push it into the corners with a toothpick.

For books with binder rings only:

Use an awl to pierce two holes in the wall closest to the binder rings, aligning the holes with the top ring and bottom ring. Thread an upholstery needle with yarn and draw the needle through a hole and around the binder ring three times. Knot the ends of the yarn on the outside of the compartments. Repeat at the other end of the spine. For extra strength, add a droplet of hot glue over each knot.

5. Assemble Compartments

Measure across the box, from wall to wall. With the craft knife and ruler, cut two strips of balsa wood measuring the box width by the depth of the "walls" (Figure C). Hot glue the balsa strips into place along the pencil lines and allow to set.

Measure the distance between the top of the box and the dividing wall below it; then measure the distance between the bottom of the box and the dividing wall just above it (these should be the same measurement). With craft knife and ruler, cut four strips of balsa measuring the length of the compartment by the depth of the "walls" (Figure C). Hot glue each piece in place along the pencil lines and allow to set.

6. Decorate Compartments

Paint the top edges of each compartment using acrylic paint and a small brush. Allow to dry before closing the cover of the book.

Cut four pieces from the sewing pattern paper to cover the exterior walls of the box. Brush glue onto the exterior balsa wall and cover with a coordinating piece of pattern paper, smoothing into place with your fingers. Repeat for all 4 outer walls. Note: If you are using a book with binder rings, you will only cover the top, bottom, and outer walls.

7. Make Pincushion

Measure the dimensions of one of the inner compartments. Cut a square of cotton fabric 2 ½ times this size. Fold the fabric into quadrants. Then cut an arc along the two open sides. Open the fabric circle. Leaving a 3" tail and beginning on the right side of the fabric, stitch around the circumference of the circle, about ¼" in from the edge and end at the right side of the fabric. Remove the needle from the thread and pull both thread tails to gather the fabric into a round pouch. Don't cinch completely closed—through a small opening, stuff the pouch with fiberfill, being sure not to make it too dense. Pull the thread tails and knot the ends. Hot glue the cushion into its compartment with the knotted side down.

JOURNAL

Journaling is, by nature, a personal experience, so why not take it to the next level by making your own journal? For the materials, you'll need a book that speaks to you—one, perhaps, with a beautiful cover or a thoughtful subject—and some paper for the pages. Consider using different types of paper to suit the journal's purpose. For example, I made one with drawing paper in one half and watercolor paper in the other, then inserted two pages from the original book (titled Part I and Part II) as section dividers. And in the journal shown at left, I glued the original cover's spine onto the opening page. The rings used to bind this book are helpful in case you'd like to add or remove pages over time.

Materials

Hardcover book

Decorative paper (optional)

Paper, for the journal pages
  Note: The amount of paper needed will depend on the thickness of the journal you'd
  like to create. For writing and sketching,
  consider using drawing paper, parchment
  paper, or tinted pastel papers. For art
  mediums such as watercolors, charcoals, or
  colored pencils, I like to use a heavier stock
  paper, such as 90-lb watercolor paper.

Two 1½" binder rings

Tools

Craft knife

Cutting mat

Pencil

Metal ruler

White glue and glue brush

Bone folder

3 rubber bands

3 clamps

Masking tape

Scrap wood

Drill and ³⁄₁₆" drill bit

Scissors

1. Remove Book Block

Using a craft knife and following the instructions on page 13,
remove the book block and set aside. Lay the book flat on a cutting mat and cut along the gutters on either side of the spine to
remove the front and back covers (Figure A). Discard the spine or
save it for another project.

2. Cover Inside of Book (Optional)

If you do not like the endpapers on the inside cover of your book,
cover them with decorative paper following the instructions on
page 15 (otherwise move on to Step 3).

3. Cut Journal Paper

Measure the height and width of one of the inside covers, as
shown in Figure B, then subtract ¼" from each measurement.
This will be the size of your journal pages. With the craft knife,
ruler, and cutting mat, cut through several sheets of journal paper
at a time to create pages of this size. Cut as many pages as are
needed to achieve the thickness you want. I like my journals to be
¾" to 1" thick.

4. Assemble Journal

When all the pages are cut, stack them up and square the corners
neatly by tapping the edges with the flat side of the bone folder.
Fasten two rubber bands around the width of the stack and one
around the length (Figure C). Center the stack on the inside of the
back cover, aligning the edge of the book block with the spine
edge of the cover. Put the top cover on top of the stack, aligning
it with the book block and back cover, and clamp the stack on
three sides.

5. Drill Holes in Journal

Place small pieces of masking tape next to the spine, near the top
and bottom of the front cover. Measure ⅜" from the spine and 1
½" from the bottom and top of the book, marking on the masking
tape with a pencil (Figure D). Set the journal on a workbench or
on top of a piece of scrap wood, and drill through the covers and
paper with a ³⁄₁₆" drill bit. Remove the masking tape and insert the
binder rings into the holes. Remove the clamps and snip off the
rubber bands with scissors.

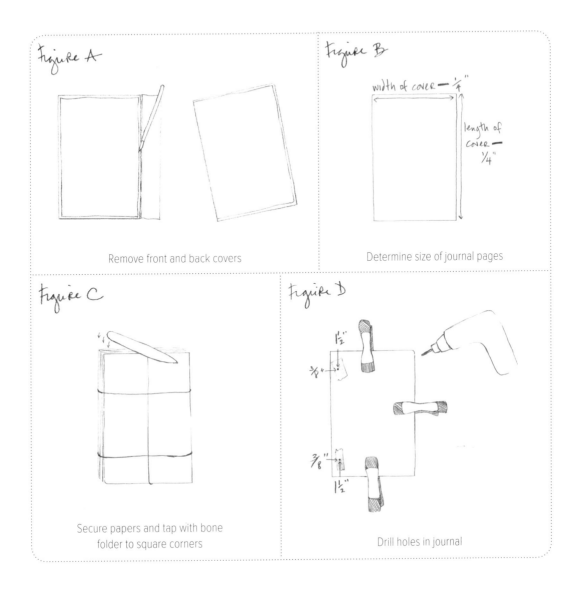

figure A

Remove front and back covers

figure B

width of cover — ¼"

length of cover — ¼"

Determine size of journal pages

figure C

Secure papers and tap with bone folder to square corners

figure D

1½"

¾"

3⁄8"

3⁄8"

1½"

Drill holes in journal

HANGING MIRROR

As I designed the projects for this book, I kept coming back to the idea of biographies and how they are, in essence, a reflection of a person. Naturally, the idea for my hanging book mirror was conceived with this self-reflective notion in mind. Picking a book for this project can be as fun as making it—a biography is an obvious choice, but any book with an alluring cover or fetching title works just as well.

Materials

Hardcover book, approximately 5" x 8"

12" length of ⅜"-wide grosgrain ribbon

Mirror, approximately 3½" square

Two 4" x ⅝" mending plates

Screws, shorter than half the thickness of your book

Tools

White glue and glue brush

Pencil

Metal ruler

Craft knife

2 clamps

Awl

Screwdriver

1. Find Book's Center

Open the book to its center page and mark it. You should have an equal number of pages on the left and the right.

2. Create Hanging Loop

Beginning on the left side of the book, flip ⅛" of pages to the right. Brush glue onto the entire page and center one end of the ribbon about 3" down from the book's top edge. Flip the ⅛" of pages back and press the pages together. Glue the other end of the ribbon to the other side of the book in the same way (Figure A). Turn the pages back to the center point and allow to dry completely, with books (or other weighted objects) on top for pressure.

3. Cut Slot for Mirror

With the book still open to its center point, turn it over so that the outside covers are facing up. Flip open the back cover (which will be on the left side) and place your mirror on the last page of the book. The mirror will ultimately peek out of a hole that you will cut in the back cover, so position it on the page where you would like it to appear on the back cover. Trace around the mirror with pencil, then measure ⅛" to either side of the mirror and mark the new width. Draw lines extending from the sides of the traced rectangle up to the top of the book (Figure B). With a craft knife and ruler, cut the rectangle up to the top edge of the book, cutting about ⅛" into the book block (or deep enough for the mirror to lie flat when inserted).

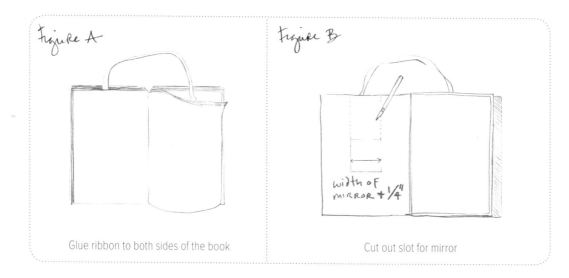

Figure A

Glue ribbon to both sides of the book

Figure B

width of mirror + ¼"

Cut out slot for mirror

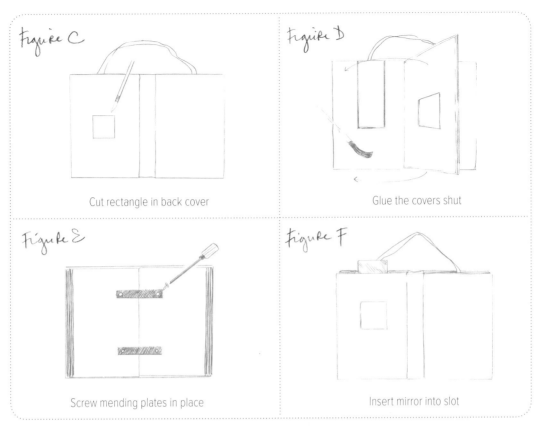

Figure C — Cut rectangle in back cover

Figure D — Glue the covers shut

Figure E — Screw mending plates in place

Figure F — Insert mirror into slot

4. Cut Window for Mirror

Flip the last page of the book—the one you just marked and cut—so it lies against the inside back cover of the book. Trace the sides and bottom edge of the cut-out rectangle. Align your mirror with the traced top and sides and trace a line across the top of the mirror to complete the rectangle. Then draw another rectangle inside of the traced shape, ¼" from all edges. Cut the smaller rectangle shape out of the cover with the craft knife and ruler (Figure C).

5. Glue Covers

Brush glue onto the last page of the book to coat the side facing the back cover and avoiding the cut-out slot. Close the cover and press down (Figure D). Open the front cover and brush glue on the first page of the book. Close the cover and press down. Allow the covers to dry fully.

6. Glue Book Block

Keeping the book open to its center point, flip the book over so the pages are facing up. Clamp each side of the book pages together and brush glue all around the outer edges of the book block, pushing glue into the crevices of the pages for secure adhesion. Allow to dry completely.

7. Install Mending Plates and Mirror

With the inside of the book facing up, center the mending plates over the spine, with one positioned near the top of the book and the other near the bottom (Figure E). Hold each plate in place and make a small hole with the awl through the screw holes in the plates. Secure the plates with screws, using the screwdriver. The mending plates will keep the book open and flat when it is hanging.

Slip the mirror into the slot and hang your completed mirror by its ribbon (Figure F).

BIOGRAPHICAL BRACELET

This bracelet uses basic materials to create a very un-basic piece of jewelry. It makes a thoughtful gift for a loved one, since you can personalize the bracelet by cutting out adjectives or phrases from loose book pages that describe the person who will wear it. I like to use really distinctive words or phrases as I think they make the most interesting bracelets.

Materials

Loose book pages (6 or more)

Wooden bangle bracelet

Acrylic paint (tube or bottle) in the color of
   your choice

Tools

Cutting mat

Craft knife

Metal ruler

Pencil

½"-wide flat-bristle brush

Mod Podge

Palette or old saucer

Paper towel

1. Select Words for Bracelet

Select words or phrases from loose book pages that make you think of the person who will be wearing this bracelet. Set the page on a cutting mat and remove the words using a craft knife and ruler. Make sure you have enough words to encircle the bangle when lined up end-to-end (Figure A).

2. Cut Strips to Cover Bracelet

Cut approximately ten 1"-wide strips from the remaining pages. To figure out the length needed for each strip, multiply the width of the bracelet times two. For example, if I were covering a 2"-wide bracelet, I would need 4" lengths of 1"-wide strips (Figure B).

3. Decoupage Strips on Bracelet

With a brush, apply Mod Podge to both sides of a 1" section of the bangle, then brush Mod Podge onto one of the strips of paper. Position the strip on the outside of the bangle and wrap the edges around to the inside. Brush more Mod Podge over the outside of the strip.

Work around the bracelet, applying strips in the same way until the entire bangle is covered. Be sure to slightly overlap each strip as you glue it in place to prevent gaps (Figure C). Clean the brush thoroughly with water and air dry. Let the bracelet dry completely.

4. Paint Bracelet

Pour or squeeze a small amount of paint onto a nonporous surface such as a palette or an old saucer. Put a sparing amount of paint on the brush, dabbing off any excess on a paper towel. Coat the outside of the bangle only, applying paint thinly so that the type on the page is still visible (Figure D). Let dry completely.

5. Decoupage Selected Words and Phrases

With the brush, apply Mod Podge to the backside of your descriptive words and phrases and stick them in place. The words should be centered along the circumference of the bracelet and aligned end to end, with a small space between each piece of paper. Brush more Mod Podge over the words (Figure E). Let dry completely.

Apply a final coating of Mod Podge on the entire outside surface to seal. Let dry completely.

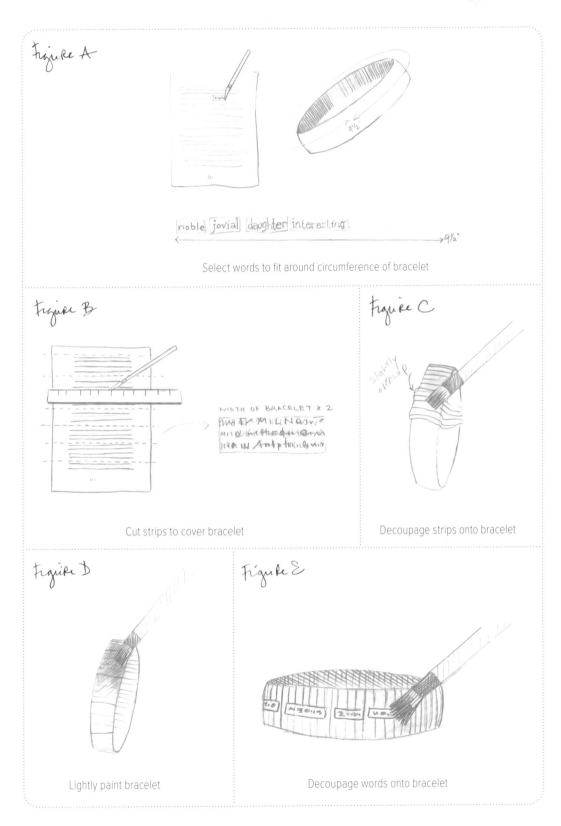

figure A

noble | jovial | daughter | interesting |

9½"

Select words to fit around circumference of bracelet

figure B

WIDTH OF BRACELET X 2

Cut strips to cover bracelet

figure C

slightly overlap

Decoupage strips onto bracelet

figure D

Lightly paint bracelet

figure E

Decoupage words onto bracelet

Story Time Clock

by Jim Rosineau

I'm always delighted when I can take a beautiful book off the shelves and put it on display. In this project, artist and furniture designer, Jim Rosineau, came up with a perfect way to do this—by repurposing a book into a clock. A title that mentions time (like the one I've used here) is a natural choice, but don't limit yourself to the theme. You could choose a cover for its typography or simply because the color goes with your kitchen.

There are all sorts of ways to personalize this project. You can stencil numbers onto the book, or create a clock face out of paper and glue it in place. Or you could attach a small feather to the second hand to illustrate that "time flies." For my clock, I painted the hands the same color as the book so they wouldn't distract from the title, but otherwise kept it simple, since the title says it all.

Materials

Hardcover book, at least 1" thick

2 ³⁄₁₆"-square quartz clock movement and hands (available at craft supply stores)

2 drywall screws, slightly shorter than the book's width

Picture hanging wire or ribbon

Tools

Pencil

Awl

Craft knife and replacement blades

Metal ruler

Clamp

White glue and glue brush

Cutting mat

Drill and ³⁄₁₆" bit

Scrap wood

Adjustable wrench

1. Pick Placement of Clock

Decide where you want the clock face to sit on the front cover of the book. Mark the center of the clock placement with a pencil. Use an awl or small drill bit to make a hole at this spot, drilling through the cover and into the first few pages of the text block.

2. Mark Placement of Clock Movement

Open the front cover. Using a ruler and pencil, measure and mark a 2 ½" square on the loose endpaper, around the clock's center point (Figure A). This will be large enough to accommodate a standard 2 ³⁄₁₆" quartz clock movement.

3. Cut Hole in Book Block

Run a craft knife along the perimeter of the square to make the hole, using a ruler for accuracy. I tend to cut through about 4 pages at a time, so cutting through the entire book block can take a little while. Flip over the pages as you cut, and clamp them to the front cover. Redraw your square and keep cutting. To maintain accurate cuts, press down firmly on the uncut pages with your other hand when cutting (Figure B). As you cut, be sure that the corner edges meet at 90-degree angles, producing a nice, clean edge. Change blades often to maintain clean cuts.

4. Cut Hole in Back Cover

Once you've cut through the entire text block, trace the square onto the inside back cover with a pencil. Place the book on a cutting mat and, using the craft knife and ruler, cut out this shape from the back cover. (This is so you can reach the clock move-

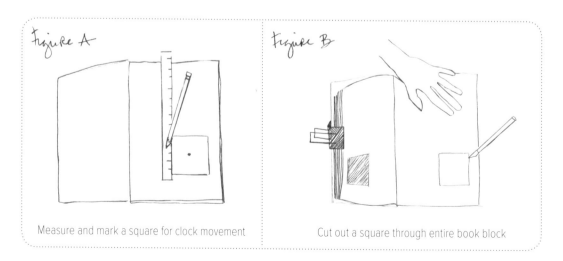

| Measure and mark a square for clock movement | Cut out a square through entire book block |

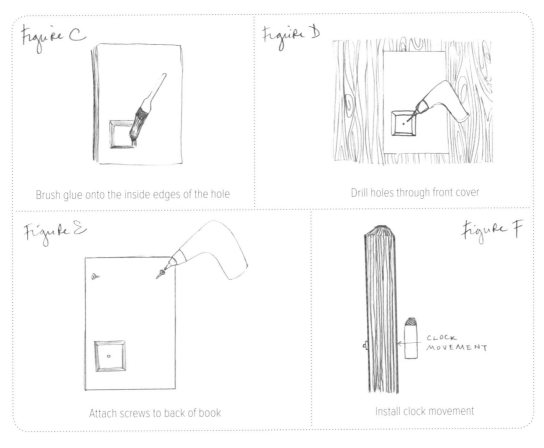

Figure C

Brush glue onto the inside edges of the hole

Figure D

Drill holes through front cover

Figure E

Attach screws to back of book

Figure F

CLOCK MOVEMENT

Install clock movement

ment when you need to set the time or change the battery.)

5. Secure Book with Glue

Brush glue onto the first and last pages of the book (the endpapers) and press them to the inside covers. Brush glue liberally around the interior edges of the cutout hole (Figure C). Close the book and clamp it shut, leaving it facedown on a clean surface. (If you leave it faceup, excess glue will puddle on the back of the book, which will be visible.)

6. Drill Hole for Clock Stem

Once the book is dry, lay it facedown on a piece of scrap wood. Using a drill and a $\frac{3}{16}$" drill bit, press the book down firmly and drill a hole into the front cover (in the spot where you made a hole in Step 1 with the awl) (Figure D). By drilling into scrap wood you minimize shredding on the front of the book.

7. Attach Picture Hangers

With the book still facedown, drill two small holes on either side at the top of the book. Insert screws and drill into place until they extend $\frac{1}{8}$" from the back cover (Figure E). These screws will help hold the book together—they should be long enough to penetrate most of the pages, but not long enough to extend out through the front cover. Wrap picture-hanging wire or ribbon around the screws for hanging.

8. Insert Clock

Insert the clock movement into the carved hole and install according to the manufacturer's instructions with provided washer and nut (Figure F). Tighten just past finger tight with a small adjustable wrench.

Mount clock hands according to the instructions provided with the movement. Insert the battery, set the proper time, and hang.

Book Ledge

This simple, stacked book ledge brings a whimsical aesthetic to any room and is a sweet spot to display a beloved knickknack. The project works best using five books in graduated sizes, all of which share a theme. I chose the books shown here for their color—I couldn't resist grouping a series of greens. This is a very easy project, though you will need to use a band saw to cut one of the books down to size. If you're not familiar with power tools, have a friend with band-saw know-how help you with this step!

Materials

5 books of graduating lengths

Two 2 ½" corner braces

Four ½" wood screws (#6)

Tools

Pencil

Metal ruler

Craft knife

Awl

Screwdriver, or drill and $3/32$" drill bit

White glue and glue brush

15 clamps

Band saw

Liquid Nails

1. Stack Books and Attach Braces

Stack the books from shortest to longest (Figure A). Pull out the third book in the stack and open its pages about one-third of the way through. Place the two corner braces equally spaced on the open book pages, with the edge of each brace flush with the outer edge of the book block (Figure B). Make sure the upright angle of the brace extends at least 1½" above the top of the book when the book is closed (Figure C).

Open the book to the page with the braces and trace around each brace with a pencil. With a ruler and craft knife, cut the rectangular shapes from the book's pages until they are approximately ⅛" deep. Place the braces into the cut-out rectangles, making sure that they lie flat, and insert the awl through the holes in the braces to make small holes in the book pages. Insert the wood screws into the holes and screw the braces into the book block with a screwdriver or drill.

Brush glue onto the front and back endpapers and press the covers closed. Then brush glue along the outer edges of the book, pushing it into the crevices of the pages for a secure hold. Attach clamps to the sides of the book and allow to dry.

2. Glue Book Blocks

Glue the rest of the books closed, brushing glue on the first and last pages of the book (the endpapers) and pressing them to the inside covers. Then brush glue along the outer edges of each book, as in Step 1. Clamp all books closed and allow to dry.

3. Cut Book

Lay the largest book on a work surface and measure 2" from the spine; mark this line along the front cover with a pencil. Using a band saw, cut the book along this line (Figure D). You will only need the piece with spine.

4. Glue Books Together

Use Liquid Nails to glue the smallest book (book #1 at the bottom of the stack) to the next book in the stack (book #2). Make sure that the outer edges of both books are flush so that the finished structure will lie flat against the wall. Repeat this step to attach book #3 (the one with the braces) to book #2, and book #4 to book #3. Set the stack on a stable surface, with the largest book on the bottom, and weight it with more books, allowing it to dry overnight.

5. Attach Book Spine and Hang

Use Liquid Nails to glue the spine portion that was cut in Step 3 to the largest book at the top of the glued stack. Align the cut edge along the back edge of the stack, leaving ⅛" between the braces and the cut edge (Figure E). (This is to leave room for the nail heads when you hang it on the wall.) Allow to dry and mount on a wall.

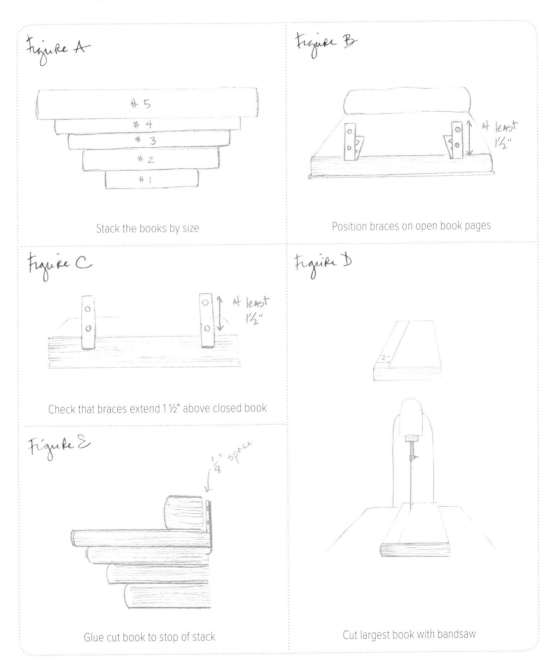

figure A

5
4
3
2
1

Stack the books by size

figure B

At least 1½"

Position braces on open book pages

figure C

At least 1½"

Check that braces extend 1 ½" above closed book

figure D

2"

Cut largest book with bandsaw

figure E

¼" space

Glue cut book to stop of stack

Best-Seller Bookshelf

A book about repurposing books would hardly be complete without a bookshelf project. I used three neutral-colored books of the same width to make this simple shelf and added a dash of color by painting the corbels a vibrant green. Throw in some hardware, and you've got yourself a masterpiece.

Materials

Spray paint, for corbels

Two 5" wooden shelf corbels

Thirty-two ¾" wood screws (#6)

3 hardcover books of the same width and thickness

Eight 6" mending plates

Tools

12 clamps

White glue and glue brush

Pencil

Craft knife

Metal ruler

Awl

Screwdriver, or drill and ³/₃₂" drill bit

Liquid Nails

1. Paint Corbels

In a well-ventilated area, spray paint corbels in a color of your choice. Allow to dry for a few hours.

2. Glue Book Blocks

Fold the front and back covers of each book so they meet and clamp them together. Then secure the three outer edges of each book block with large clamps. Generously brush glue on all three sides of each book block, moving the clamps as needed (Figure A). Let the brush bristles sink into the crevices between the pages to make sure they fully adhere. Keep the books clamped and let dry overnight.

3. Cut Holes for Mending Plates

Arrange the books end-to-end in a pleasing order with the spines facing the same direction. Open the front covers of two adjacent books and place two mending plates across the gap. Trace around the plates with pencil then set the plates aside. Using a craft knife and ruler, cut out the traced rectangles, cutting about ⅛" deep into the book block (Figure B).

Repeat this step with the second and third books.

4. Attach Front Mending Plates

Place the mending plates into the four cut-out rectangles bridging the three books. Insert the awl through the holes in the plates to make small holes in the book pages. Then insert the wood screws into the holes and screw the braces into the book block. Brush glue onto the endpaper of the inside cover of all three books and press the covers closed (Figure C).

5. Attach Back Mending Plates

Gently turn over the three attached books and open the back covers. Attach four more mending plates as you did in Step 4 and glue the back covers closed. Allow to dry for an hour.

6. Attach Corbels

Lay the three attached books, front covers facing down, on a work surface. Run Liquid Nails along each corbel's top edge and place one at each short end of the shelf, making sure that the back of the corbel is flush against the edge of the shelf (Figure D). Press down firmly and allow to dry overnight. Hang the shelf from the hanging slots on the back of the corbels.

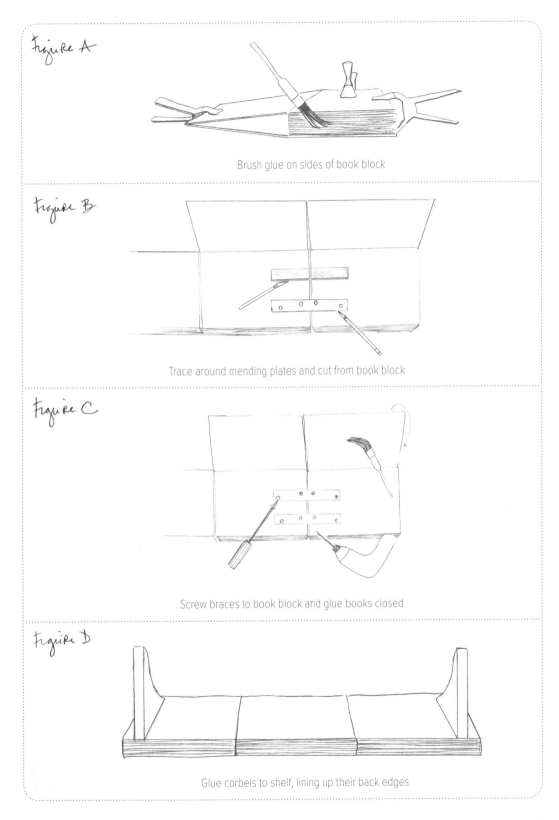

Figure A

Brush glue on sides of book block

Figure B

Trace around mending plates and cut from book block

Figure C

Screw braces to book block and glue books closed

Figure D

Glue corbels to shelf, lining up their back edges

BIRDHOUSE

For this project, I turned a birdhouse into a book house fit for any bibliophile. An opened book serves as a roof for this tiny home, with pages from the book papering its walls. While it isn't suited for outdoor use, it adds a bit of whimsy to any bookshelf. A string through the roof allows you to hang it from the ceiling, which is especially charming in a kid's bedroom.

Materials

Hardcover book, approximately 7" x 9"

18" x 24" sheet of foam core

A cylindrical object (such as a pencil, chopstick, or knitting needle), for the perch

Tools

Metal ruler

Cutting mat

Pencil

Craft knife

White glue and glue brush

Clamps

Heavy-duty upholstery thread and craft needle (optional)

Awl

Masking tape

Bone folder

Glue gun and glue sticks

Note: The instructions provided here are based on using a 7" x 9" book, though you can alter the instructions to suit a book of any size. Simply determine the pitch of the roof that you would like to make and adjust the dimensions of the "walls" for your project.

1. Determine Pitch of Roof and Width of House

Stand the book upright and open it so that the pages are evenly divided between the front and back. Looking at the triangle formed by the open pages, decide which angle feels right for your "roof." Measure the width between front cover and back cover, 1½" from the covers' top/front edges (Figure A). This will determine the pitch of the roof and the width of the house.

2. Determine Height of Front/Back Walls

To determine the height of the front/back walls, add 3" (for the roof peak) to the width measurement determined in Step 1, then add another 2"-3" (for the front/back wall) (Figure B). In the example shown, the front/back wall including the roof peak is 10" tall and 5" wide.

3. Create Front and Back of House

Lay the foam core onto a cutting mat. Using a ruler and pencil, measure and mark the front and back wall dimensions (10" tall x 5" wide) onto the foam core. Draw a parallel line 3" below the top edge of the rectangle; this will be the top of the wall. Then mark the center of the top edge of the rectangle; this will be the roof peak. With a ruler and pencil, draw a line from the roof peak to the top of the wall on either side of the rectangle (Figure C). With a ruler and craft knife, cut out the wall piece. Trace around this shape onto another section of foam core and cut it out to create a second wall.

4. Create Side Walls

The height of the side walls is the same as the height of the front/back, omitting the roof peak measurement. (In the example shown, the height of the side walls is 7".)

To determine the width of the side walls, subtract 2" from the height of the book you are using for the roof, which allows for a 1" overhang on either end (Figure D). (In the example shown, the length of the side walls is 7".)

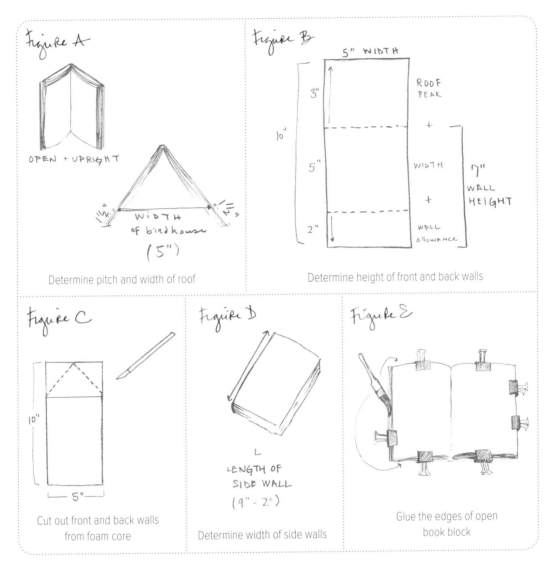

figure A

OPEN + UPRIGHT

WIDTH
of birdhouse
(5")

1½"   1½"

Determine pitch and width of roof

figure B

5" WIDTH

3"

10"

5"

2"

ROOF PEAK

+

WIDTH

+

WALL allowance

7"
WALL HEIGHT

Determine height of front and back walls

figure C

10"

5"

Cut out front and back walls
from foam core

figure D

L
LENGTH OF
SIDE WALL
(9" - 2")

Determine width of side walls

figure E

Glue the edges of open
book block

5. Select Pages to Cover Walls

Now go through the book and seek out pages you find especially appealing, such as illustrated pages or chapter openers; these will cover the outside of the house. Gently run your craft knife along the book's gutter to remove these pages. Make sure you have enough pages to cover all the walls, plus extra for the base (which we'll create in Step 10). Set the pages aside.

6. Glue Book Block

To make the roof stable, you'll need to glue the book block. Brush glue on the inside back and front covers and press closed. Then open the book to its center again, with an equal number of pages at the front and back of the book. Clamp the front pages to the front cover and the back pages to the back cover. Generously brush glue around all three outer sides of the front of the book, being sure to push glue into the crevices of the book block (Figure E). Move the clamps as needed to glue every spot. Then brush glue around all three outer sides of the back of the book. Leave the clamps on and allow to dry overnight.

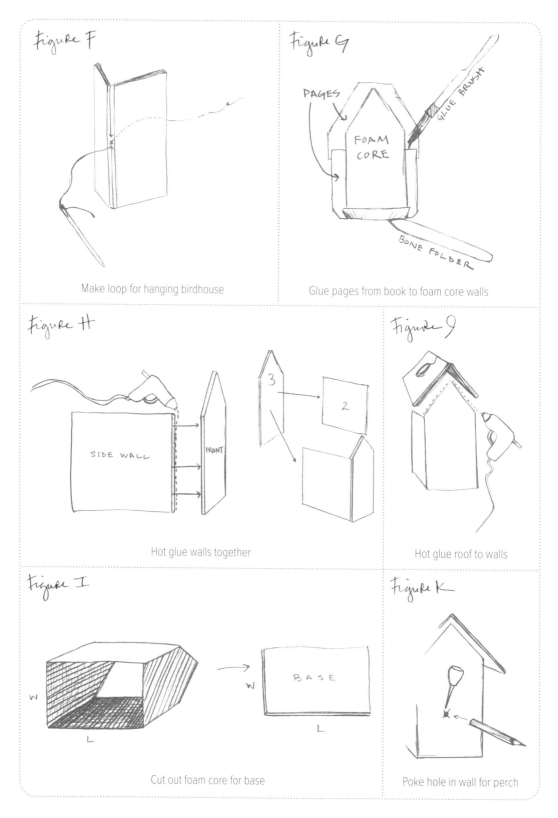

Figure F

Make loop for hanging birdhouse

Figure G

PAGES

FOAM CORE

GLUE BRUSH

BONE FOLDER

Glue pages from book to foam core walls

Figure H

SIDE WALL

FRONT

3

2

Hot glue walls together

Figure J

Hot glue roof to walls

Figure I

W

L

W

BASE

L

Cut out foam core for base

Figure K

Poke hole in wall for perch

7. Make Loop for Hanging (Optional)

If you would like to hang your house, you will need to attach a hanging loop. When the glue on the book is completely dry, measure and mark the center of the spine's length from the outside. With an awl, punch a hole through the spine to the inside of the book. Thread the craft needle with approximately 36" of heavy-duty thread, making a large knot at its tail. Thread the needle through the hole on the inside of the spine and make a 2"-3" loop on the outside of the book for hanging (Figure F). Secure the loop with a double knot. Coil the string and secure it with a piece of masking tape to keep it from tangling while you finish the house.

8. Wallpaper the House

Lay out the four foam core walls for the front, back, and sides of the house, with their right sides facing up. Using the pages you set aside in Step 5, decide which page you would like to use to cover each wall (note that you may need more than one page for this). Leave an extra ½" of paper to wrap over the edges of the boards. Brush glue on the back of the page and press to the foam core. Use a bone folder to smooth the page, then wrap excess paper securely around the edges of the foam core (Figure G). Wallpaper all the boards and allow to dry.

9. Assemble the Structure

Heat up the hot glue gun. Run hot glue along the vertical edge of one of the side walls and attach it to the inside edge of the front wall, making sure the walls meet at a right angle (Figure H). Repeat with the other side wall, attaching it to the other inside edge of the front wall. Then run hot glue on the two remaining side wall edges and attach to the back wall.

10. Make the Base

Once the four walls are in place, measure the length and width of the bottom of the house (measuring from the outside edge of the foam core walls) and cut a piece of foam core to this size (Figure I). With glue and glue brush, wallpaper the outside of the foam core base with a page you selected in Step 5. Once the paper on the base has dried, run hot glue along the bottom edges of the house structure, and set the house on top of the base.

11. Attach the Roof

Run hot glue along the top edge of the front and back peaks (Figure J). Firmly place the roof on top of the house, making sure that the overhang is equal on both sides. If there are any gaps between the roof and the wall, reinforce with a drop of hot glue.

12. Attach Perch and Hang the House

I used a vintage clown head for the perch shown here, though you can use any cylindrical item you like, such as a chopstick, knitting needle, or a small twig. Get creative with this aspect, using the subject of your book as a guide. Decide how far you want the perch to protrude from the house, then add 1"; cut your perch to this measurement. Pick a spot for your perch on the front wall and punch a hole with the awl, widening the hole so that the perch fits snugly. Put a dab of hot glue on the edge of the hole and slide the perch in about an inch (Figure K).

Unwrap the coiled string and hang the house.

BOOK ADORNMENTS

Book Tattoos, Bookplates, Dust Jacket & Beauty Bookmark

The projects presented here are all about adorning the books that you love. The Book Tattoos (shown at top left) are a clever way to spruce up and customize a book by rubber-stamping the edges of its book block. The Bookplates (shown at top right) are an elegant way to claim ownership of your library. The Dust Jacket (shown at bottom left) is great for protecting a cover (or concealing the subject matter) of a beloved book—the packing tape used to cover the jacket not only holds it together but also makes it waterproof. And the Beauty Bookmark (shown at bottom right) features an embedded mirror in the spine of a book so you can check your smile while seemingly engrossed in an intruiging passage. I hope that all these adornments help you treasure the books you love to read.

Book Tattoos

Materials

Hardcover or paperback book

Rubber stamps, alphabet or various designs and motifs (small enough to stamp the edges of the book)

Ink pad or broad-tipped marker, one or more colors

Tools

2 – 4 clamps (size depends on the thickness of the book)

Masking tape

1. Secure Covers (Hardcover Book Only)

If tattooing a hardcover book, fold back the front and back covers and clamp them together to hold in place.

2. Secure Book Block

Because the outer side edge of a book block can be uneven, I prefer to tattoo along the top and bottom edges of the book block (the surface between the spine and outer book edge); these ends are typically flush and will accept ink from the stamp more evenly. To create a smooth surface, clamp the book block near the area where you plan to stamp (Figure A).

3. Plan Your Design and Stamp

Before you start stamping, decide on your design, keeping in mind the size of the book, the scale of the stamps, and how much surface area you would like to decorate. Here are some design suggestions to get you started:

> Use a large stamp, but let the design fall off the edge of the book block, giving it a cropped effect (Figure B).

> Create an all-over random pattern, using two or three different small stamps and ink colors (Figure C).

> Create a repeating design with a simple pattern, but repeat it with different ink colors.

> Using alphabet stamps, spell out the book owner's name or initials, a saying, or a greeting (Figures D and E).

> For perfectly aligned text or patterns, place masking tape along the book block and stamp just above the line.

Apply ink to your stamp by pressing it to your ink pad or coloring the raised surface of the stamp with a broad-tipped marker. Press the stamp to the book block edge firmly, but don't rock back and forth—that can cause the print to distort.

Allow the ink to dry for 15 minutes, then remove the clamps.

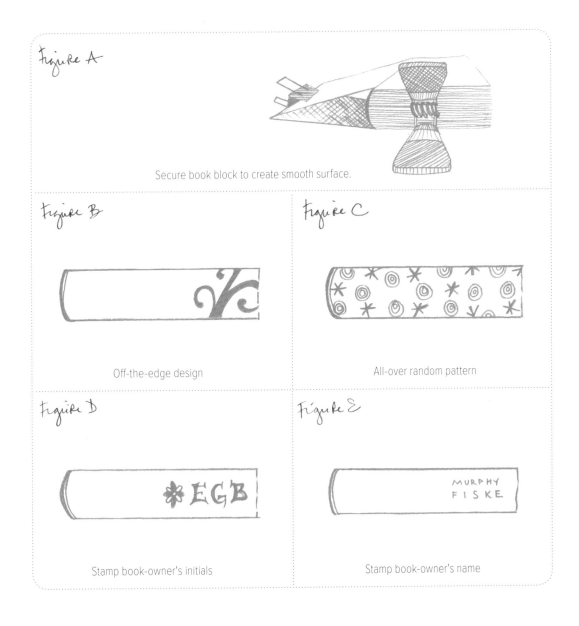

Figure A

Secure book block to create smooth surface.

Figure B

Off-the-edge design

Figure C

All-over random pattern

Figure D

Stamp book-owner's initials

Figure E

Stamp book-owner's name

BOOKPLATES

Materials

6 illustrated book pages, at least 4" x 3"

6 pieces of transparent vellum, at least 4" x 3"

Ink pad or broad-tipped marker, one or more colors

Rubber stamp with a design, for your motif

Rubber alphabet stamps, for lettering

Tools

Cutting mat

Pencil

Metal ruler

Craft knife or scissors

Masking tape

Scrap paper

Gluestick

Bone folder

Pen or marker

1. Cut Pages and Vellum

On a cutting mat, trim six book pages and six pieces of vellum to 4" tall by 3" wide.

2. Stamp Motif

Lay out one of the vellum sheets vertically. Apply ink to your motif stamp by pressing it to your ink pad or coloring the raised surface of the stamp with a broad-tipped marker. Center the stamp over the top half of the vellum and press firmly, but don't rock back and forth—that can cause the print to distort.

Repeat on the five remaining pieces of vellum. Change ink colors if you'd like, cleaning the stamp between prints

3. Stamp Words

Lay the vellum on the cutting mat, lining it up squarely with the grid lines. (Since the vellum is transparent, you'll be able to see the lines through it.) Use masking tape to secure the corners of the vellum to the cutting mat (Figure A).

Pull out the letters E, X, L, I, B, R, S from your alphabet stamps. Apply ink to the letter stamps and stamp "EX LIBRIS" on the vellum, using the grid lines from the cutting mat to keep your lines straight. Start stamping at the center and work out toward the edges. Repeat on the other five vellum sheets. Let all six pieces dry completely before handling, so you don't smudge them. Note that vellum is less absorbent than other papers, so the ink will need a minute or two to dry.

4. Glue Vellum to Book Page

When dry, pair each vellum piece with a cut book page, checking that the book page design is compatible with the stamped vellum design. Place the vellum sheet facedown and apply gluestick to the backside, working from the center out to the edges (Figure B). Place the glued side of the vellum on top of one of the cut book pages, aligning the top edges and corners first (Figure C). Press together and turn over. Drag a bone folder over the bookplate in a few different directions to fuse the pieces together. Repeat with the five remaining pairs.

5. Sign and Paste into Book

Using pen or marker, write the book owner's name beneath "EX LIBRIS." Apply gluestick to the back of the bookplate and paste to the endpaper on the inside front cover of a book.

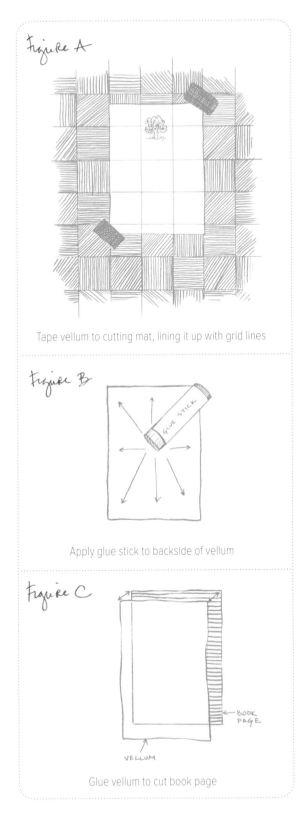

figure A

Tape vellum to cutting mat, lining it up with grid lines

figure B

GLUE STICK

Apply glue stick to backside of vellum

figure C

← BOOK PAGE

VELLUM

Glue vellum to cut book page

Here are some design variations to try out on your bookplates:

> Instead of stamping once, try a random repeat pattern with your motif stamp.

> Use a larger motif stamp and let the design fall off the edges for a cropped effect.

> Turn the bookplate to make it horizontal.

> Instead of using markers, print the owner's name with alphabet stamps.

> Place your vellum over book pages with type instead of illustrations.

> Glue your finished bookplates to 3" x 4" adhesive mailing labels—this is especially useful if the bookplates are a gift.

Dust Jacket

Materials

Book, to cover with dust jacket

Loose book pages from a different book (12 - 15 pages, depending on the size of your book and the size of the page)

Clear packing tape

Tools

Metal ruler

Pencil

Gluestick

Craft knife or scissors

Cutting mat

Bone folder

1. Measure Your Book

Using a ruler, measure the height (H), width (W), and depth (D) of the book you intend to cover. Then calculate the size of the dust jacket by following this formula:

H + 3" = Height of dust jacket

[(W x 2) + D] + 4" = Width of dust jacket

This formula will create a dust jacket with approximately 2"-wide flaps.

For instance, if your book measures 8"H x 5"W x 1"D, your formula would be:

8" + 3" = 11" height of dust jacket

[(5" x 2) + 1"] + 4" = 15" width of dust jacket

2. Design Dust Jacket

Gather loose book pages from any book or books you want to use. Pages can all be from a single book, or you can mix it up with pages of different size or tone, or go with a theme, like pages from a cookbook.

Next, lay out the pages to fit the measurements determined in Step 1. (It's okay if the dust jacket is a little larger than it needs to be at this phase—you'll trim it down to size in Step 3.) You can arrange the pages any way you like, such as in a grid pattern, diagonally, or haphazardly. Each page will need to overlap by ¼" so work this allowance into your final measurements. Consider the placement of any wording, titles, or illustrations you might find significant—you may want to center these details on the front cover (right side) of the dust jacket, leaving space for the flap.

3. Glue Dust Jacket Together

Once your pages are arranged in a pleasing manner that is as large or larger than the dimensions of the dust jacket, tack the pieces together by running gluestick along the edges of each page and overlapping it on the neighboring sheet by ¼". Press firmly into place. Once all of the pages are glued together, the sheet will probably be a little larger than you need it to be. Using scissors or a craft knife, ruler and cutting mat, trim the jacket to its proper size.

4. Tape Dust Jacket Together

Working carefully, lay strips of clear packing tape over the front side of the dust jacket in even rows, extending a bit beyond the edges. Overlap each row of packing tape by ¼" and press into place as you go to prevent bubbles and wrinkles (Figure A). (Note: you can apply the tape in any pattern—horizontally, vertically, diagonally, etc.—just be sure all the paper is covered by the tape.)

Once the dust jacket is fully laminated with packing tape, turn it over and trim the excess tape off the edges with a craft knife or scissors (Figure B).

5. Cover the Book

With the dust jacket still facedown, measure 2" from the top and bottom edges and crease by running a bone folder along the edge of a ruler (Figure C). Fold along these creases.

Center the spine of the book that you wish to cover on the dust jacket. Working on the back cover first, fold the extra length of dust jacket (approximately 2") vertically over the edge of the book cover to create a sleeve. Crease with a bone folder and slip the back cover into the sleeve (Figure D). Repeat to create a sleeve for the front cover.

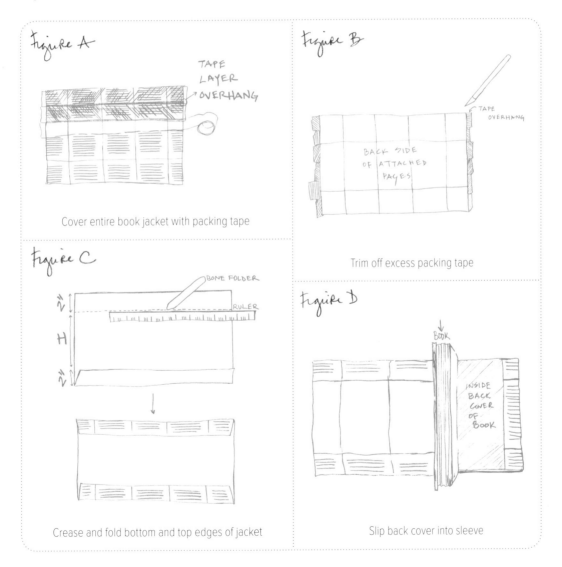

Figure A

Cover entire book jacket with packing tape

Figure B

Trim off excess packing tape

Figure C

Crease and fold bottom and top edges of jacket

Figure D

Slip back cover into sleeve

Beauty Bookmark

Materials

Hardcover book, with spine at least 1½" wide

⅛"-thick cardboard, same dimensions as book spine

Heavy cardstock, same dimensions as book spine

⅛"-thick mirror, 1" wide and 1" to 3" tall (depending on size of spine)

Ribbon or tassel (optional)

Beads, pom-poms, or sequins (optional)

Tools

Craft knife

Metal ruler

Cutting mat

Pencil

White glue and glue brush

Bone folder

Awl or nail (for embellishment only)

1. Remove Spine and Prepare Bookmark

Using a craft knife and following the instructions on page 13, remove the book block and set aside. Open the cover and lay it on a cutting mat. Cut the spine from the back and front covers. Reserve the rest of the book for another project.

Measure the length and width of the spine, then cut one piece each of the same size from the cardboard and cardstock (Figure A). Set the cardstock aside. Sparingly brush glue onto the cardboard and adhere it to the back of the book spine. Place several books on top of the bookmark to press the layers together and let dry for at least 20 minutes. Once the bookmark is dry, use the craft knife to trim any excess cardboard from the spine so all edges are smooth.

2. Place Mirror in Bookmark

The size of your mirror will depend on the space available on the book spine—pick one that is the right size to fit this space. Position the mirror on the front of the spine where you want it to appear and lightly trace around it with a pencil. Score the outlined shape with the blade of the craft knife until the shape is cut out cleanly (Figure B).

3. Assemble Bookmark

Turn the spine over so that the backside is facing up. Position the mirror in the cut-out space, reflective side down. Brush glue onto the wrong side of the cardstock and place over the spine. With the bone folder (or your fingers), press firmly and smooth out the cardstock. Place several books on top of the bookmark to press the layers together and let sit for at least 20 minutes (Figure C).

4. Embellish Bookmark (Optional)

With the right side facing up, measure the center of the bookmark's width, then measure ¾" down from the top (adjust these measurements depending on the design of your book's spine). With an awl (or a large nail) make a hole at this point. Loop a ribbon or tassel through the hole, embellish with beads or a pompom, and knot off to finish. In the example shown, I used ¼"-wide grosgrain ribbon for the tassel and stitched five mirrored sequins onto the ribbon (as a play on the mirror theme).

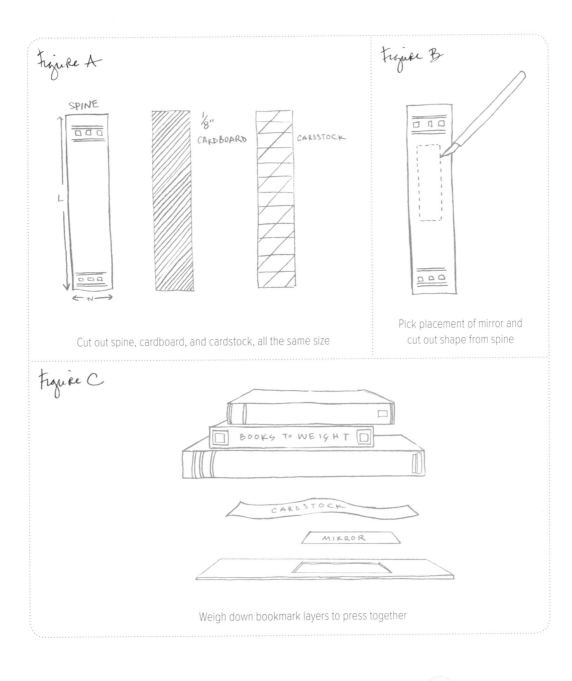

Figure A

SPINE

1/8" CARDBOARD

CARDSTOCK

Cut out spine, cardboard, and cardstock, all the same size

Figure B

Pick placement of mirror and cut out shape from spine

Figure C

BOOKS TO WEIGHT

CARDSTOCK

MIRROR

Weigh down bookmark layers to press together

LETTERED WREATH

For this modern take on the classic wreath, I made paper rosettes from book pages and sculpted them into a circular form. Because this project requires 200 rosettes, I recommend doing it as a group activity; with cocktails and conversation, you'll have the rosettes finished in no time. I like to fashion this wreath out of a mix of pages from different sources for their varying tones and textures. It's a great way to make use of book blocks and pages left over from other projects.

Materials

Loose book pages (approximately 10)

24-gauge wire or floral wire, cut into 5"
  lengths (approximately 220)

8" wire wreath form

Two 10" lengths of string or yarn

Tools

Craft knife

Metal ruler

Cutting mat

Masking tape

Scissors

Pencil

Small piece of cardboard

Glue gun and glue sticks

Scissors

MAKING THE PAPER ROSETTES

1. Trim Pages

A single page will make one rosette. Try using different-sized pages to make a variety of flower sizes. For pages that contain lines of text, use a craft knife, ruler, and cutting mat to trim off the outer margin from one side of each page so the text comes right up to the edge (Figure A). This will be the part of the rosette that shows in the finished product

2. Wrap Rosettes

Lay your index finger an inch or so from the bottom edge of the page, on the untrimmed side. Wrap the page snugly around your finger and hold in place (Figure B).

Wrap the rest of the page over and around your index finger, encasing your middle finger as well (Figure C). This wrap does not need to be as snug as the first wrap.

Repeat the wrap once more, this time encasing your thumb too (Figure D). This wrap does not need to be as snug as the first wrap.

3. Secure Rosettes

With your thumb, index, and middle fingers still encased within the coiled page, pinch the paper just past your fingertips, creating a rosebud shape (Figure E). Slip your fingers out of the coil and wrap wire around the pinched section to hold in place (Figure F). Twist the remaining page to create the stem.

Repeat Steps 2 and 3 to make 200 rosettes.

4. Make Rosette Pairs

Use 100 of the completed rosettes to create 50 pairs. To do this, hold two rosettes together snugly, then wrap a length of masking tape around their stems to secure. Set the 50 pairs and 100 single rosettes aside.

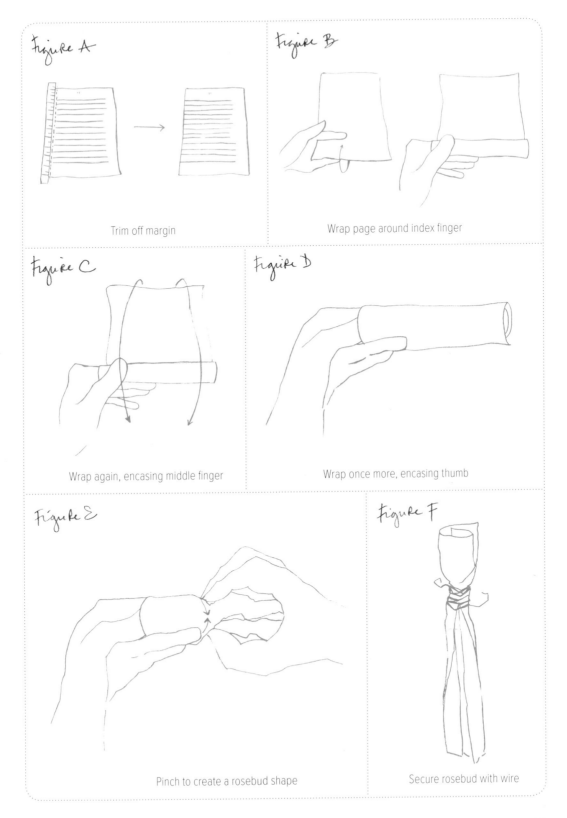

Figure A

Trim off margin

Figure B

Wrap page around index finger

Figure C

Wrap again, encasing middle finger

Figure D

Wrap once more, encasing thumb

Figure E

Pinch to create a rosebud shape

Figure F

Secure rosebud with wire

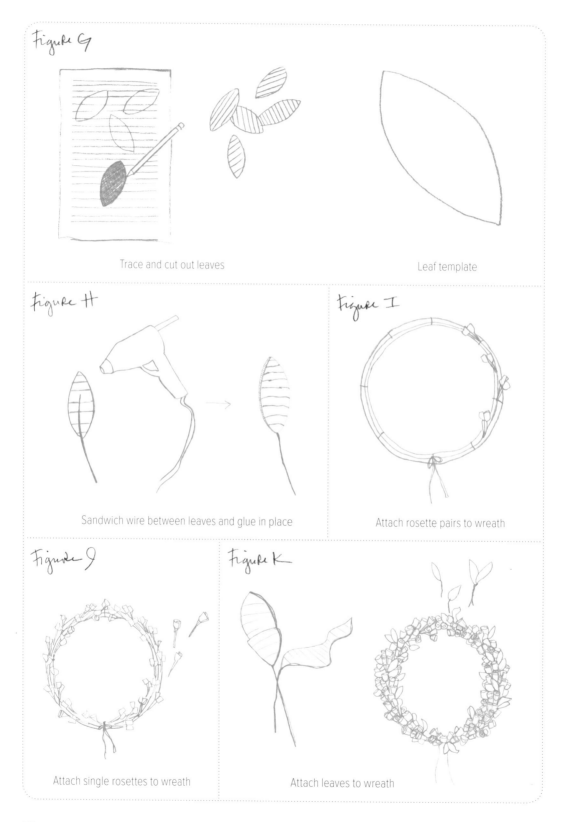

Figure G

Trace and cut out leaves

Leaf template

Figure H

Sandwich wire between leaves and glue in place

Figure I

Attach rosette pairs to wreath

Figure J

Attach single rosettes to wreath

Figure K

Attach leaves to wreath

MAKING THE LEAVES

5. Draw Leaf Template and Cut Out Shapes

Trace the leaf template at left or draw a simple leaf shape onto your piece of cardboard, sizing it appropriately to the scale of your rosette forms. Using scissors, cut out the template. (Heat up the glue gun at this point so it's ready for the next step). Create 40 leaves by using a pencil to trace around the template onto loose pages and cutting them out with scissors (Figure G).

6. Assemble Leaves

Lay a paper leaf flat on your work surface, then place a piece of wire along its center, as if it were the stem. Apply hot glue on the entire leaf and place a second leaf on top, aligning the edges and pressing together to sandwich the wire between (Figure H). Repeat until you have assembled 20 leaves.

MAKING THE WREATH

7. Attach Rosette Pairs to Wreath Form

Find the bottom of your wreath form and tie a piece of colored string or yarn to mark its placement. Attach pairs of rosettes to the wreath form with masking tape or wire (Figure I).

When attaching the flowers, it's important to be aware of the wreath's orientation, with some stems and leaves pointing down (or in the same direction) and with clusters in certain areas. There should be a sense of order and thought. As you work, keep the overall design in mind. You may wish to have an equal amount of rosettes around the wreath form, or you may prefer to create an asymmetrical design by clustering rosettes in one area.

8. Attach Single Rosettes to Wreath Form

Once the wreath form is decorated with all the rosette pairs, start attaching the 100 single rosettes (Figure J). These can be hot glued in place, as they'll rest snugly against the rosette pairs attached in the previous step. You may find you need the stems to be shorter to fit into small gaps; if so, simply cut them with scissors.

Keep adding single rosettes until you feel the wreath is full and nearly complete. You may find you have a few left over, or you might need to make a few more.

9. Attach Leaves to Wreath Form

Attach the leaves to the wreath form wherever you see fit, using their wire "stems" to hold the leaves in place (Figure K). You can also twist two or three together to create a nice grouping. These are helpful for hiding gaps in the design or filling in spots that reveal the wreath form beneath. Leaves can be attached with hot glue if the wire is too tricky to twist in the chosen spot. Bend the leaves into more organic shapes to complete the presentation.

10. Attach Loop and Hang Wreath

Cut the string from the bottom. Tie another string to the top of the wreath form on its backside and make a loop to hang on a wall or door.

THREE-BOOK CHANDELIER

This hanging light fixture, made by joining three book covers in a circle, adds a scholarly note to any setting. Choose three books of the same size with a similar subject, or simply pick three covers that look nice together. The books in the sample shown here all have a "home" theme, with covers featuring illustrations of trees, a shovel, and a house. To allow the light to come through the covers, I created a pattern of holes using a leather punch. Once the chandelier is pieced together, a simple electric lighting set is added.

Materials

3 hardcover books, 9" tall x 7" wide

3 sheets 8 ½" x 11" transparent vellum

12" wooden embroidery hoop

Three ⅜" screws (#2)

Light cord set, such as IKEA's "Hemma" (see Sources on page 142)

15 loose book pages

Thin, 26-gauge craft wire

Tools

Craft knife

Pencil and metal ruler

Plywood or old cutting board

Leather punch, with varying nib sizes

Hammer

Scissors

Gluestick

Adhesive linen bookbinding tape

Awl

Screwdriver

Clamp

Masking tape

White glue and glue brush

1. Remove Book Block

Using a craft knife and following the instructions on page 13, remove the book blocks from the three books and set aside. Repair the book's spine, if necessary (see page 14).

2. Create Hole Pattern

With the outside of the book facing up, measure to find the center of each book's back cover and lightly mark this spot with a pencil. Draw a vertical and horizontal line through this dot, making a cross. Then draw two diagonal lines from corner to corner going through the center point of the cross.

3. Punch Holes in Cover

Place the first book cover on a piece of plywood or an old cutting board with the outside of the book facing up. You will punch holes in the cover along the lines you drew in Step 2, leaving ¼" between each hole (Figure A). To make a clean hole, place the nib on the cover and hit the punch with a hammer two or three times. I began at the center of the design using the largest nib size and decreased to the smallest nib as I worked outward. Repeat this step to punch holes in the other two covers.

4. Add Scrim

When your hole pattern is complete, turn each book cover over so the outside of the book is facing down. Cut a sheet of transparent vellum to fit over the hole-punch pattern on each book, including an extra ¼" of vellum on all sides. Apply gluestick to the edges of each vellum piece and place it over the hole-punch design. Press down to secure the vellum on each book and allow to dry.

5. Tape Books Together

Lay the book covers out in a row, with the outsides of the books facing down. Cut two lengths of adhesive linen tape to the same height as the covers. Moisten the tape and lay it along the connecting edge of each book, pressing down with your fingers (Figure B). Once all three books are attached, measure their length.

In order to fit around the circumference of the embroidery hoop, the length of the connected book covers must be 43". If your length is a little short, cut a piece of mat board to use as an extender. Glue decorative paper to the mat board and use linen tape to attach it to one of the books at the end.

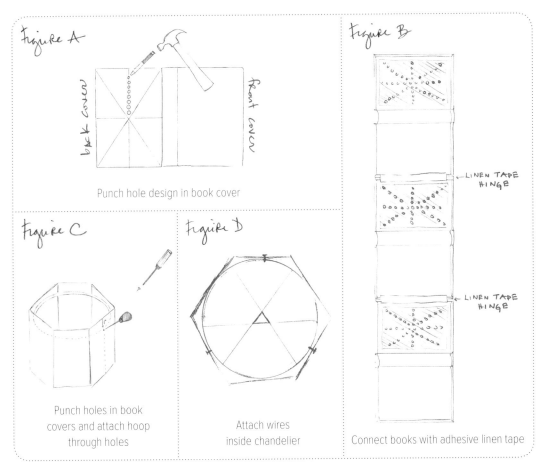

figure A

back cover

front cover

Punch hole design in book cover

figure C

figure D

Punch holes in book
covers and attach hoop
through holes

Attach wires
inside chandelier

figure B

←LINEN TAPE
HINGE

←LINEN TAPE
HINGE

Connect books with adhesive linen tape

Stand the hinged book covers upright and bring the two ends together to meet. Connect these two ends with adhesive linen tape.

6. Attach Hoop

On the outside front cover of each book, measure 1" down from the top center edge and punch a small hole with the awl. Place the inner ring of the embroidery hoop inside the chandelier and clamp in place. Reinsert the awl through each hole in the book covers to make a slight indentation in the wooden hoop. Insert the screws through each hole and screw through the book covers into the hoop (Figure C). Remove the clamps.

7. Cover Cords

Wrap the cord from the light cord set with masking tape. Cut the loose book pages into ½"-wide strips. Brush glue on each strip and wrap around the cord.

8. Attach Wire

Cut three 20" lengths of wire. Attach the wires to the hoop inside the chandelier at three equidistant points (Figure D). Pull the wire taut across the diameter of the hoop and wrap tightly around the opposite edge. All three wires, when attached, will create a triangle in the center of the chandelier.

9. Insert Light Cord and Hang

Thread the plug of the light cord set through the wire triangle, from bottom to top, until the light socket is resting within the triangle. Wrap an additional 12" length of wire around the cord and its surrounding wires to hold the light socket securely to the wire triangle. Insert a 40-watt bulb into the light socket. To hang, screw a cup hook into the ceiling and drape the cord over the hook to the desired height.

Two-Book Luminary

This project is the simplified sequel to the Three-Book Chandelier on page 72. It is an uncomplicated yet urbane form and works great as a dining table centerpiece or evening light on the porch. All you need are two books of the same size and a candle encased in glass.

Materials

2 hardcover books, 8" tall x 5" wide

3 sheets 8½" x 11" transparent vellum

Candle in glass container (I like to use a
   4"-wide jar candle)

Tools

Craft knife

Cutting mat

Pencil

Metal ruler

White glue and glue brush

Bone folder

Plywood or old cutting board

Leather punch, with varying nib sizes

Hammer

Gluestick

Adhesive linen bookbinding tape

1. Remove Book Block

Using a craft knife and following the instructions on page 13, remove the book blocks from both books and set aside.

2. Strengthen the Spine

Lay the book covers flat with the insides facing up. Remove two pages from one of the book blocks and cut two 2½" strips from the text column on each page (not the margin). Brush glue on the backside of one of the strips and place it over the inside of the book's spine (Figure A). Run a bone folder over the paper to press into place, pushing the paper into the crevices of the spine. Attach the second strip to the other book in the same way.

3. Create Hole Pattern

With the outsides of the book covers facing up, measure to find the center of each front and back cover and lightly mark this spot with a pencil. Draw a vertical and horizontal line through this dot, making a cross. On the back covers, lightly trace three circles within each other at the center point of the cross, measuring 3½", 2½" and 1¾" in diameter. On the front covers, trace the smallest circle only at the center point of the cross (Figure B).

4. Punch Holes in Cover

Place the first book cover on a piece of plywood or an old cutting board with the outside facing up. With the leather punch and a hammer, punch holes in the cover along the lines you drew in Step 3, leaving ¼" between each hole (Figure C). To make a clean

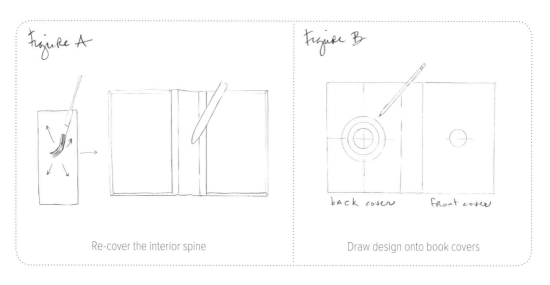

| Re-cover the interior spine | Draw design onto book covers |

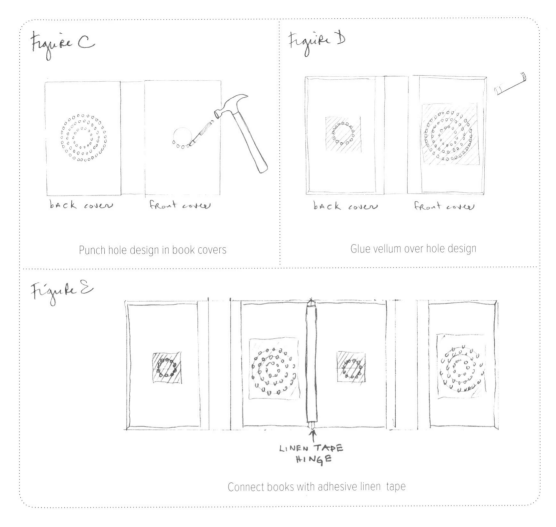

Figure C

back cover front cover

Punch hole design in book covers

Figure D

back cover front cover

Glue vellum over hole design

Figure E

LINEN TAPE
HINGE

Connect books with adhesive linen tape

hole, place the nib on the cover and hit the punch with a hammer two or three times. I began with the largest nib size for the outer circles and decreased to the smallest nib size for the smaller circle. Repeat this step to punch holes in the other book cover.

5. Add the Scrim

When your hole pattern is complete, turn each book cover over so the outside of the book is facing down. Cut a sheet of transparent vellum to fit over the hole-punch patterns on each book, including an extra ¼" of vellum on all sides. Apply gluestick to the edges of each vellum piece and place it over the holes (Figure D). Press down to secure and allow to dry. Repeat with the other covers.

6. Tape Books Together

Lay the book covers side by side, with the outside of the book facing down. Cut a length of adhesive linen tape the same height as the covers. Moisten the tape and lay it along the connecting edge of the two books, pressing down with your fingers (Figure E).

Stand the book covers upright and join the other two ends, forming a square. Cut a second length of adhesive linen tape and secure the open edge. Place a candle inside the luminary and light.

BOOK BURSTS

by Yvette Hawkins

The basic skills of cutting and folding come together in these complex-looking, three-dimensional forms. The instructions for the Book Bursts came from Yvette Hawkins, a UK-based artist. The sculptures are made entirely from book pages—in fact, a single 300-page book will yield four bursts, which makes a nice grouping to hang together on a wall.

Materials

Any book with at least 300 pages

Tools

Craft knife and replacement blades

White glue and glue brush (optional)

Metal ruler

Pencil

1. Deconstruct Book

If using a hardback book, follow the instructions on page 13 to remove the book block with a craft knife. Or, if using a paperback, simply cut off the front and back covers with the craft knife.

With the covers off the book block, check that it has a strong spine and that it has been glued rather than sewn. (When a spine has been sewn, you can see the stitched threads along the spine.) If the spine is sewn—or if it just seems weak—generously brush glue on the spine to strengthen it. Let the glue dry completely before proceeding.

2. Measure and Mark Text Block

With the book block facing up, measure the height of the first page and divide it by four. Draw lines across the width of the page to define the quarters, extending these lines across the spine. Score the spine with a craft knife along these lines (Figure A).

3. Cut Out Sections

Use the craft knife and the metal ruler to cut through the text block where you have drawn your lines (Figure B). To make accurate cuts, use a smooth cutting motion without applying too much pressure. As you slice deeper into the book's pages, fold back the pages that you have already cut so that it is easier to cut precisely (Figure C). You may find it helps to remeasure and redraw your line as you proceed. Repeat this step until all four sections have been divided. Note that it takes some time to complete this step and that you may need to change your craft knife blade if it gets dull.

4. Create Book Bursts

When the book block has been divided into four pieces, start folding the pages to create the bursts. Each book block section will create one burst.

Fold the first page of the first book block section in half so that it meets the spine edge (Figure D). Flip to the next page, folding it the same way, then folding it in half again (Figure E).

Repeat these two folds until you have folded the entire text block. You will see an alternating pattern emerge as you keep folding

(Figure F). Once you have reached the middle of the text block, it may be easier to flip it over and start folding from the other side.

Fold the other three book block sections in the same manner.

5. Assemble Book Bursts

To finish a book burst, bring the first page to meet the last page, creating a round form. Hammer a nail in the wall and hang the burst from the hole in its center (where the spine has bent back).

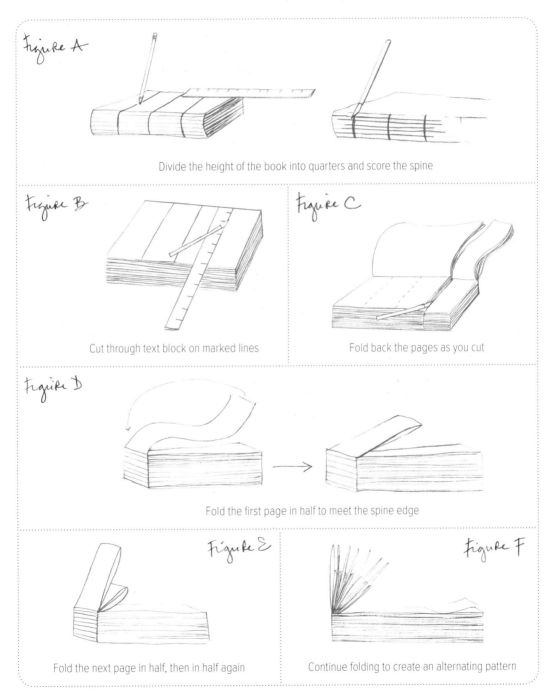

Figure A

Divide the height of the book into quarters and score the spine

Figure B

Cut through text block on marked lines

Figure C

Fold back the pages as you cut

Figure D

Fold the first page in half to meet the spine edge

Figure E

Fold the next page in half, then in half again

Figure F

Continue folding to create an alternating pattern

KINDLE KEEPER

For the avid reader, a Kindle—or any e-reader, really—is a pretty compelling gadget. And though the content a person downloads makes each Kindle unique, the truth is that they all look alike. And perhaps the most vital experience an e-reader denies is the feel of a book in your hands.

To beautifully marry the traditional with the modern, I've created this Kindle Keeper, which is a nifty way to personalize your e-reader while protecting it from the elements. I made mine specifically to suit a Kindle, but it's a cinch to customize for any e-reader—or even a BlackBerry or other electronic device—by choosing your book size accordingly.

Materials

Hardcover book, roughly 8½" tall x 6" wide x ½" thick (or approximately 1" taller and wider than the device you'd like to cover)

3 pieces adhesive Velcro

Two 8½" x 11" pieces decorative paper

Bookplate (see page 60) or library pocket (see Sources on page 142)

Tools

Craft knife

Metal ruler

Pencil

Cutting mat

White glue and glue brush

Bone folder

1. Remove Book Block

Using a craft knife and following the instructions on page 13, remove the book block and reserve it for another project.

2. Cover Inside Spine

Lay the book cover flat, with the inside facing up. Measure the spine's height and width, then add ½" to the width; cut a piece of decorative paper to these measurements. Brush glue onto the backside of the paper and press into place on the spine (Figure A). Use a bone folder to smooth the paper into the crevices of the spine so it lies flat. Allow to dry.

3. Cover Endpapers (Optional)

If you do not like the endpapers on the inside cover of your book, cover them with the decorative paper as well, following the instructions on page 15 (Figure B).

4. Attach Kindle and Bookplate

Apply three pieces of adhesive Velcro to the back of the Kindle (two at the top and one at the bottom; Figure C). Attach the hook/loop mate to each piece of Velcro, then remove the paper backing. Center the Kindle on the inside back cover, pressing down to secure the Velcro to the back cover (Figure D).

If desired, attach a bookplate (see page 60) or library pocket to the inside front cover of your "book."

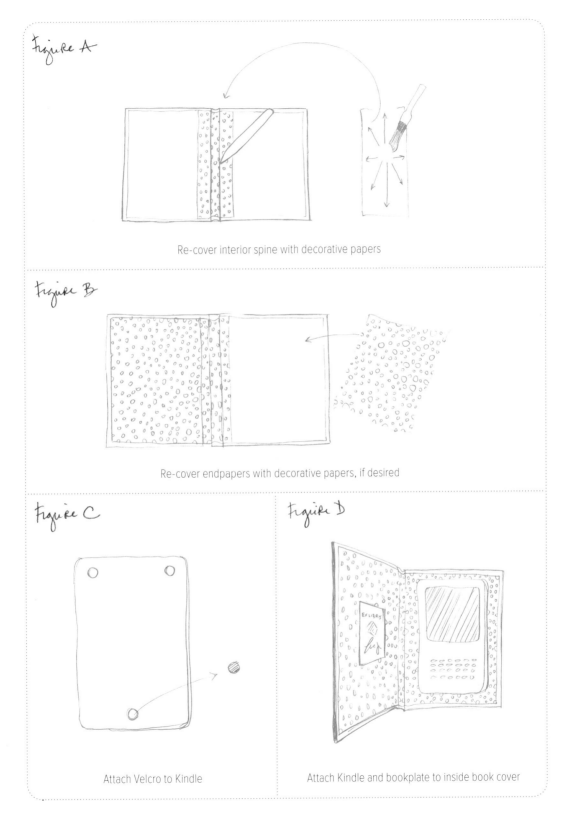

Figure A

Re-cover interior spine with decorative papers

Figure B

Re-cover endpapers with decorative papers, if desired

Figure C

Attach Velcro to Kindle

Figure D

Attach Kindle and bookplate to inside book cover

Novel Firescreen

When weather warms up and a toasty hearth is no longer needed, sometimes it's nice to conceal the empty fireplace alcove with a decorative screen. Here, I used cut-up books to create a front support to prop up an elegant panel. The screen not only hides the hearth, but creates a *trompe l'oeil* optical illusion, in which books seem to emerge from behind it. This is a fairly simple project, though you do need a band saw to cut the books. If you don't already own a band saw (or know how to use one), you'll need a friend who can help you out.

Materials

½"-thick medium-density fiberboard (MDF), cut to 24" x 30"

25 loose pages (from one book)

Two 8" metal shelf brackets

Sixteen ½" wood screws (#6)

8 hardcover books

Three 2½" corner braces

Tools

White glue and glue brush

Bone folder

Mod Podge

Metal ruler

Pencil

Awl

Screwdriver

Band saw

Craft knife

Clamps or weights

Glue gun and glue sticks

1. Arrange and Glue Pages

Lay the MDF flat on the ground. Arrange loose pages on the board in rows, staggering the placement to create a tiling pattern (see the photo on page 89). Leave 1½" of extra paper at both edges of each row so you can wrap the pages around the board. Brush glue onto the back of each page, one at a time, and press in place on the MDF, smoothing out the page with a bone folder. Continue until all the pages are glued into place. Then brush Mod Podge over all of the pages on the front of the board to protect and seal them. Allow to dry completely.

2. Attach Brackets

Lay the screen front side down. Measure 6" in from each side and mark with a pencil. Brush glue on the backside of each bracket and press into place along the marked lines (Figure A). Make sure the bottom of the bracket is flush with the bottom edge of the board so it will stand straight when turned upright (the brackets will act as feet). Once the glue is dry, use the awl to punch holes through the screw holes on each bracket and twist screws into place with a screwdriver.

3. Cut Books

You will cut all eight books width-wise (from spine to outer edge) into 16 uneven halves. To do so, measure and mark a line across each book where you want the cuts to be placed. Starting at the spine edge, run the books through the band saw.

4. Create Support Base

Choose three of the larger book halves for the bottom of the support base on the front of the screen. Open each book about ⅓ way through and place a corner brace in the center of the page, along the width of the book (Figure B). Be sure the straight edge of the brace is flush with the edge of the book's pages, then trace around the shape of the brace. Set the brace aside. With a craft knife, cut out the rectangular shape from the pages, cutting about ⅛" deep into the book block. Place the corner brace in the carved rectangle (it should lie flush in the book). Using the awl, punch holes through the screw holes in the brace. Then attach the brace using screws and screwdriver. Close the book. Repeat with the other two book halves.

5. Glue Book Blocks

Brush glue onto the endpapers at the front and back of all 16 book halves. Close the covers and press down. Generously brush glue onto the outer edges of each book, starting at the top and working down the side. Let the brush bristles sink into the crevices between the pages to make sure they fully adhere. Close each book and secure all three sides with clamps (or place weights on top of each book). Allow to dry completely.

6. Attach Braces and Extra Books

Set the screen on a table, with pages facing up, so that the bracket legs hang off the table's edge and the screen lies flat. Evenly space the three book halves with the corner braces along the bottom edge of the screen, making sure that they are flush with the bottom edge (Figure C). Use the awl to make holes in the screw holes in the corner braces, then attach the braces with screws and a screwdriver.

Stand the firescreen up on its braces. Arrange the rest of the book halves in stacks on top of the brace books and hot glue into place, stacking books as you desire.

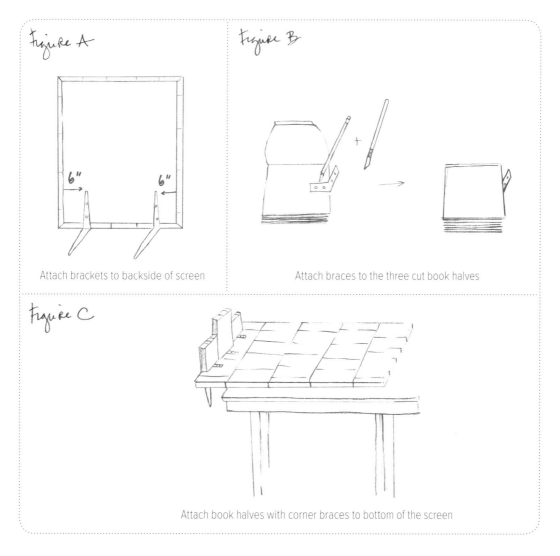

figure A

6"   6"

Attach brackets to backside of screen

figure B

Attach braces to the three cut book halves

figure C

Attach book halves with corner braces to bottom of the screen

MATCHBOOK

I combined a book and an upside-down drawer pull to create this charming fireside match holder. I love the way the tree design on the book I used abstractly relates to the wooden matchsticks as well as the logs on the fire. If you like, you can also paint the drawer pull and its screws with a metal paint to coordinate with the book.

Materials

Hardcover book

14" length of ½"-wide ribbon

Cup-shaped drawer pull (plus accompanying
    screws)

Tools

Metal ruler

Pencil

White glue and glue brush

3 clamps

Drill and drill bit slightly smaller than your
    screws

Screwdriver

1. Attach Ribbon

Open the book to the inside back cover. On the loose endpaper facing the back cover, measure and mark two spots: 1" from each side edge and 2" from the top. Brush glue on the marked areas and press the ends of the ribbon onto the glue, making sure the ribbon isn't twisted. The ribbon will make an upside down U shape, creating a loop above the book (Figure A).

2. Glue Book Block

Brush glue on the entire inside back cover of the book and close the book. Flip the book over and open the front cover. Brush glue on the entire inside front cover and close the book. Generously brush glue on all three sides of the book block. Let the brush bristles sink into the crevices between the pages to make sure they fully adhere. Clamp the book on three sides and let it dry overnight (Figure B).

3. Attach Drawer Pull

Position your drawer pull upside down on the front cover of the book, forming a cup. Make sure to choose a spot for the drawer pull that works well with the cover's design. With a pencil, mark where the screw holes will be. Remove the drawer pull and predrill these marked holes. Put the drawer pull back in place, aligning it with the drilled holes, and twist screws into place with a screwdriver (Figure C). Note: If the drawer pull you're using can't be screwed into place from the front, simply glue it into place with superglue.

Hang the Matchbook by its ribbon from a nail in the wall.

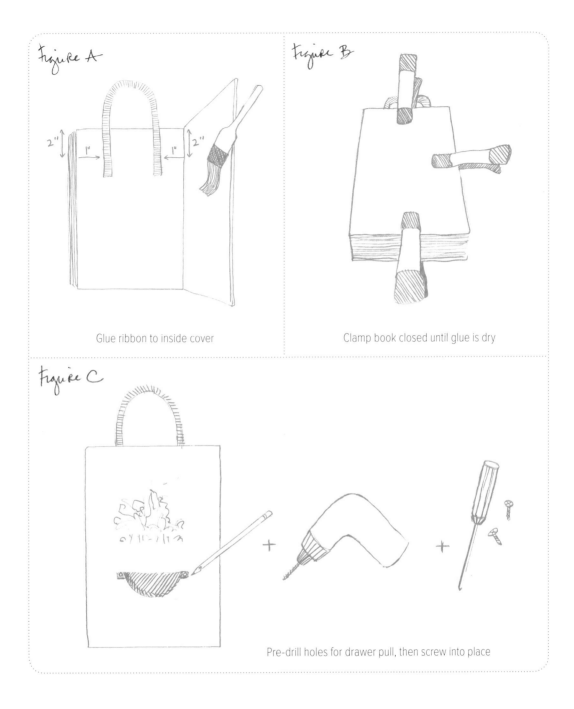

figure A

2"
1"
1"
2"

Glue ribbon to inside cover

figure B

Clamp book closed until glue is dry

figure C

+ +

Pre-drill holes for drawer pull, then screw into place

ORNAMENTS

Writer's Blocks, Wordy Birds & Bookish Ornaments

I love to decorate trees, windowsills, and even doorknobs with ornaments made from repurposed books, and here are three of my favorites. The three-dimensional, star-shaped Bookish Ornaments (shown at top left) are made from cut-out pieces of a book cover and folded book pages. The Wordy Birds (shown at bottom) are made using simple origami embellished with some frosty, light-catching sequins. And the Writer's Blocks (shown at top right) are a great way to showcase a favorite element from a book, such as a poem, story, recipe, or even a vintage illustration.

WRITER'S BLOCKS

Materials

A few loose book pages (for 1 block)

Wooden block: 1" square for small size or 2" square for large size

Small screw eye, ⅛" diameter

14" length of ⅞"-wide ribbon

Tassel (or other embellishment)

Tools

Cutting mat

Pencil

Metal ruler

Craft knife

White glue and glue brush

Awl

Glue gun and glue sticks

1. Cut Squares for Blocks

Lay a loose book page on your cutting mat. Place your block on the loose book page, centering it on a design detail that you would like to feature. Trace a square around the block and cut out the shape using a ruler and craft knife. Pick three other spots from the loose sheets and cut out those shapes, as well. For the top and bottom of the block, trace a shape that is ⅜" larger than the block and cut out with a ruler and craft knife. Clip the corners of the larger squares about ⅜" from the edge.

2. Attach Squares

Brush glue onto the backside of one of the larger squares and press to the top of the block, wrapping the extra paper over the edges. Repeat for the bottom of the block (Figure A). Then apply glue to the backside of the smaller squares and press each to one of the block's sides.

3. Attach Ribbon and Tassel

Measure the center point on the top of the block and mark it with a pencil. Use the awl to create a hole at this spot, and twist the screw eye into the hole. Slip the ribbon through the eye of the screw and tie the ends in a double knot for hanging. Center the tassel on the bottom of the block and hot glue into place.

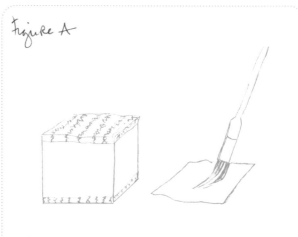

Glue larger papers to the top and bottom of the block and fold over the edges

Bookish Ornaments

Materials

Hardcover book

5 loose book pages

Note: Because you'll be folding the papers many times, you want to be sure your pages aren't brittle (otherwise they'll tear).

18" length of ¼"-wide ribbon

Tools

Cutting mat

Pencil

Metal ruler

Craft knife

Gluestick

White glue and glue brush

Clamps

Glue ribbons to book covers

1. Cut Materials

On a cutting mat, use your pencil and ruler to trace five 4" squares onto loose book pages and cut out with a craft knife. Then trace and cut out two 2" squares from the book's covers. Cut the ribbon into one 2"-long piece and two 8"-long pieces.

2. Fold Pages

Lay one paper square on a flat surface. Fold the square in half lengthwise and crease; then fold it in half widthwise and crease. Open the square flat and flip it over. Fold the lower right corner to the upper left corner and crease. Open the square flat and flip it back over to the first side. Fold again along the vertical crease so that the page folds down on itself with this pleat (Figure A).

Repeat with the remaining four paper squares.

3. Attach Pages

Decide on the order you would like your pages to appear. Using the gluestick, glue the flat outer sides of the folded squares together into a sequence, making sure that the points where the forms open are all at the same corner position. Align the edges and press the squares together as you glue. Continue gluing until all five folded squares are connected.

4. Attach Ribbons to Covers

Lay the covers side by side, ½" apart, with right sides down. Place a drop of glue ¼" from the top inside edge of both covers and press the ends of the 2" length of ribbon to the glue, bridging the ½" gap. Then glue each 8" length of ribbon to the bottom outer corners of each cover (Figure B). Allow to dry.

5. Attach Pages to Covers

Apply gluestick to the first "page" of your book and press it to the front cover, aligning the edges and making sure that the pages' open points are at the corners with the ribbons. (This is necessary for the book to open into its star shape.) Apply gluestick to the final "page" of the book, bringing the back cover up and over to meet the page. Clamp the "book" shut and allow to dry.

6. Make Star

Once the book is dry, the ornament can be displayed either as a star or as a closed book—simply open it up to reveal the star shape. Tie the ribbons into a bow to hang.

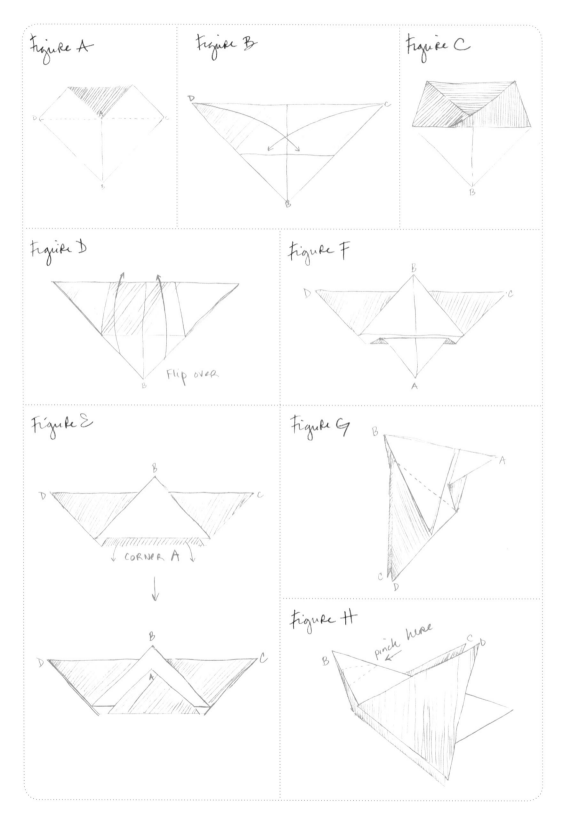

Figure A

Figure B

Figure C

Figure D

Flip over

Figure F

Figure E

CORNER A

Figure G

Figure H

pinch here

Wordy Birds

Materials

Loose book page (1 page per bird)
  Note: Because you'll be folding the paper many times, you want to be sure it isn't brittle (otherwise it'll tear).

5mm-wide sequins

Tools

Cutting mat

Pencil

Metal ruler

Craft knife

Sewing needle and thread

Glue and glue brush

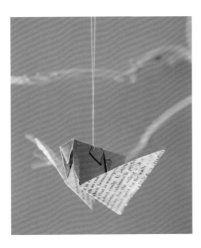

1. Cut Paper

On a cutting mat, use your pencil and ruler to trace a 5" square onto a loose page from a book, then cut out with a craft knife.

2. Make Bird

Lay the paper square on a flat surface in a diamond shape. Fold and crease the two diagonals (folding each corner to its opposite corner), and unfold.

> Fold point A to the center (Figure A).

> Fold again along the center (C to D) crease (Figure B). Fold corner D along the fold just above point B so that its point rests just beyond the center mark. Fold corner C in the same way, forming a pentagon (Figure C). Then unfold C and D, and turn over.

> Fold point B up beyond the top edge, so that the sides of B meet the creases at the top edge behind it (Figure D). Crease.

> Pull out corner A (Figure E) so that it lies on top of B.

> Fold down point A in a pleated fashion, so its folded edge meets flush with the folded edge of B (Figure F).

> Fold C back to meet D and rotate the paper counter-clockwise. Then fold C and D up along their hidden creases to create the wings (Figure G).

> To form the head, pinch pleats into the sides of point B. Pinch at the top point and invert the folds.

3. Make Hanging Loop

Thread a needle with a 12" length of thread, doubled. Insert the needle into the bird's back, between the wings. Loop and knot the thread to form a 2"-3" hanging loop

4. Attach Sequins

Brush glue onto the tips of one of the wings and attach a few sequins. Allow to dry before turning over to attach sequins to the other wing.

Music Book

by Jen Khoshbin

This musical book, designed by Jen Khoshbin, is fitted with the tune of your choice. Aside from the crank-arm protruding from the spine, the book appears untouched, so it's important to choose one with a stunning cover (or, better yet, one that matches the tune). Because the book I used here is French and "rose" is in the title, I chose "La Vie en Rose" for my melody.

Materials

Hardcover book, at least 1" thick

Music box element (see Sources on page 142)

¾" circle decorative paper or fabric (or ¼" grommet)

Tools

Large clamps

White glue and glue brush

Pencil

Metal ruler

Craft knife

Small flathead screwdriver

Drill and ¹¹/₆₄" drill bit

¼" hole punch

Glue gun and glue sticks

Bone folder

Superglue

1. Glue Book Block

Open the book's front cover and flip past a few pages. Pull back the back cover and clamp it to the front cover and first pages; keep them to the left. Clamp the remaining book block together with 2 or 3 large clamps. Generously brush glue on all three sides of the book block, moving the clamps as needed. Let the brush bristles sink into the crevices between the pages to make sure they fully adhere. Allow to dry completely, then unclamp the back cover.

2. Cut Out Rectangle for Music Box Element

With the book opened to the first page of the glued book block, use a pencil and ruler to mark a rectangle 2" high by 2½" wide on the right-hand page, ⅜" from the spine (Figure A). This is where you will make a cutout for the music box element to sit.

With your ruler and craft knife, cut through the book block to create a 1"-deep hole. Cut slowly and smoothly for clean edges. As you slice through the paper, discard the cut pieces.

3. Insert Music Box Element

Using a small flathead screwdriver, pry off the crank-arm of the music box element by lifting the small plastic pieces that hold it in place (Figure B). Insert the music box element inside the newly created hole in the book block.

4. Create Slot for Crank-Arm

With a pencil, mark the point on the inside of the hole where the crank-arm will pass through to the outside of the book's spine. Measure the exact spot of this point, and then measure and mark its corresponding spot outside on the spine. With a ¹¹/₆₄" sized drill bit, carefully drill through the outside of the spine through to the hole, creating a slot for the crank-arm (Figure C).

5. Insert and Reattach Crank-Arm

Put the music-box element in the hole in the book block.

Punch a hole in the center of the decorative paper or fabric circle with a ¼" hole punch, then slip the crank-arm through the hole (or through the grommet, if you prefer). Insert the crank-arm through the outer hole in the book's spine and into the music box element inside the book. Reattach the plastic pieces that hold the crank-arm in place in the music box element.

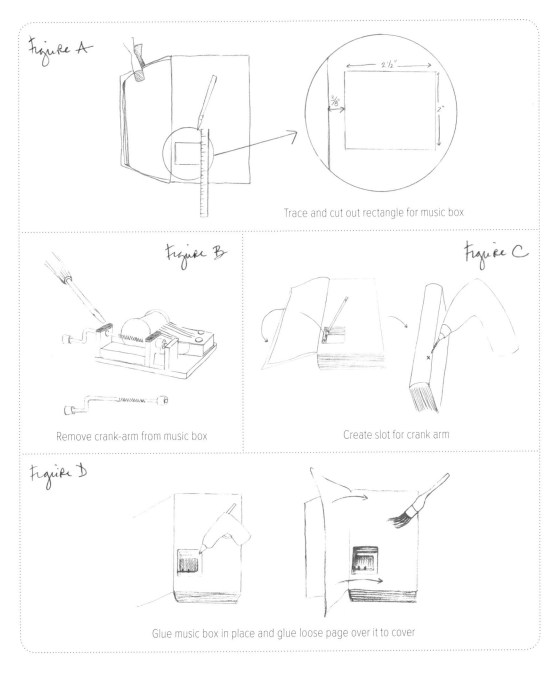

Figure A

2 ½"

⅜"

2"

Trace and cut out rectangle for music box

Figure B

Remove crank-arm from music box

Figure C

Create slot for crank arm

Figure D

Glue music box in place and glue loose page over it to cover

6. Glue Music Box in Place

Secure the music box by adding a few dollops of hot glue around its sides and at the corners. Avoid getting any glue on the inside of the music box.

To hide the music box element, brush white glue onto the page with the cut-out hole (avoiding the hole), and press the facing page over the hole (Figure D). Smooth out any air pockets with a bone folder.

Slide the decorative paper, fabric, or grommet up the crank arm to meet the hole on the spine (if using a grommet, push it into the hole), then glue into place with a drop of superglue.

LITERARY LAMP

Illuminate yourself with this one-of-a-kind lamp, simply constructed from a stack of books and a basic lamp kit from a hardware store. You'll need sturdy books for this project, so keep that in mind in addition to theme or color when you make your choice. I made my lamp from four dictionaries, turning one of the book block edges outward to highlight its intricate carved tabs.

Materials

4 large hardcover books, at least 1½" thick

Lamp kit

6" length threaded lamp pipe

Light bulb (I prefer 40 watt)

Lampshade

Tools

White glue and glue brush

12 clamps

Metal ruler

Pencil

Scrap wood

Drill and ⅜" drill bit

Craft knife

¼" dowel (or chopstick)

Liquid Nails

C-clamps or heavy books

1. Glue Book Blocks

Brush glue on the inside of the front and back covers of each book, then close the covers. Secure the three outer edges of each book with large clamps. Generously brush glue on all three sides of each book block, moving the clamps as needed (Figure A). Let the brush bristles sink into the crevices between the pages to make sure they fully adhere. Keep the books clamped and let dry overnight.

2. Drill Holes

Beginning with the book that will be on the bottom of your stack, find the center of the cover and mark it with pencil. Lay the book flat on a piece of scrap wood and drill a hole through the book at the marked spot (Figure B). Lay the next book in the stack on your scrap wood and place the drilled book on top of it. When you like the position of the next book, push a pencil through the drilled hole to mark the placement of the hole in the next book. Continue to drill holes in the next three books in this way. For a quirkier lamp (as shown in the photo on page 107, slide the books from side to side a couple of inches, rather than centering them.

3. Cut a Groove for the Cord

So that the finished lamp base will lie flat, you'll need to cut a groove in the bottom of the base for the lamp kit cord to run through. Lay the bottom book of your stack face down. Lay the cord on the base, from the hole to the book's back (outer) edge; trace along both sides of the cord with a pencil. Cut this shape out of the cover with a craft knife (Figure C). Measure the thickness of the cord and keep cutting pages from the book until you have cut a ditch deep enough for the cord to lie flat inside of it.

4. Stack and Glue Books

With the bottom book right side up, insert the dowel in the drilled hole. Slide the next book onto the dowel to determine where the two books will overlap. Lift the book and apply Liquid Nails to the cover—only in the area where the two books will touch—then slide the book back onto the dowel and press down. Continue to glue the books together this way (Figure D), then use C-clamps to squeeze them together (or weight the stack with heavy books). Allow to dry overnight. Remove the dowel.

5. Assemble Lamp

Screw the 6" length of threaded lamp pipe into the hole in the top book. Twist into the book about ½", or until it feels stable. Thread the lamp cord through the hole in the bottom of the stack and up through the lamp pipe (Figure E). Then attach the lamp kit following the package instructions. Add a bulb and shade, and you're done.

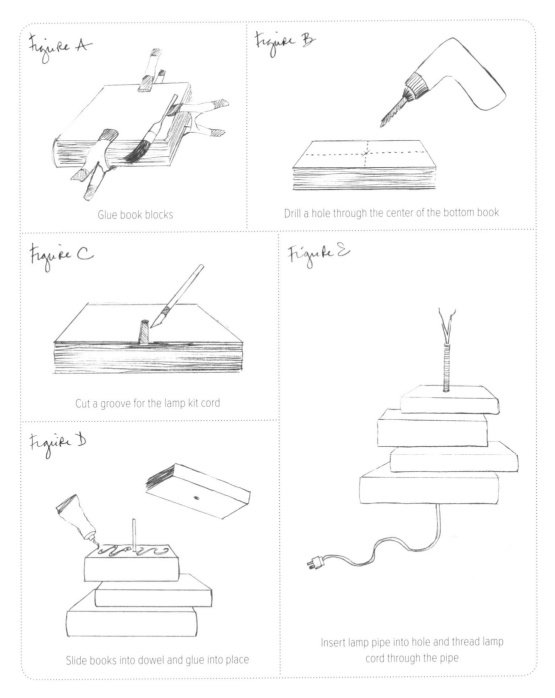

Figure A

Glue book blocks

Figure B

Drill a hole through the center of the bottom book

Figure C

Cut a groove for the lamp kit cord

Figure D

Slide books into dowel and glue into place

Figure E

Insert lamp pipe into hole and thread lamp cord through the pipe

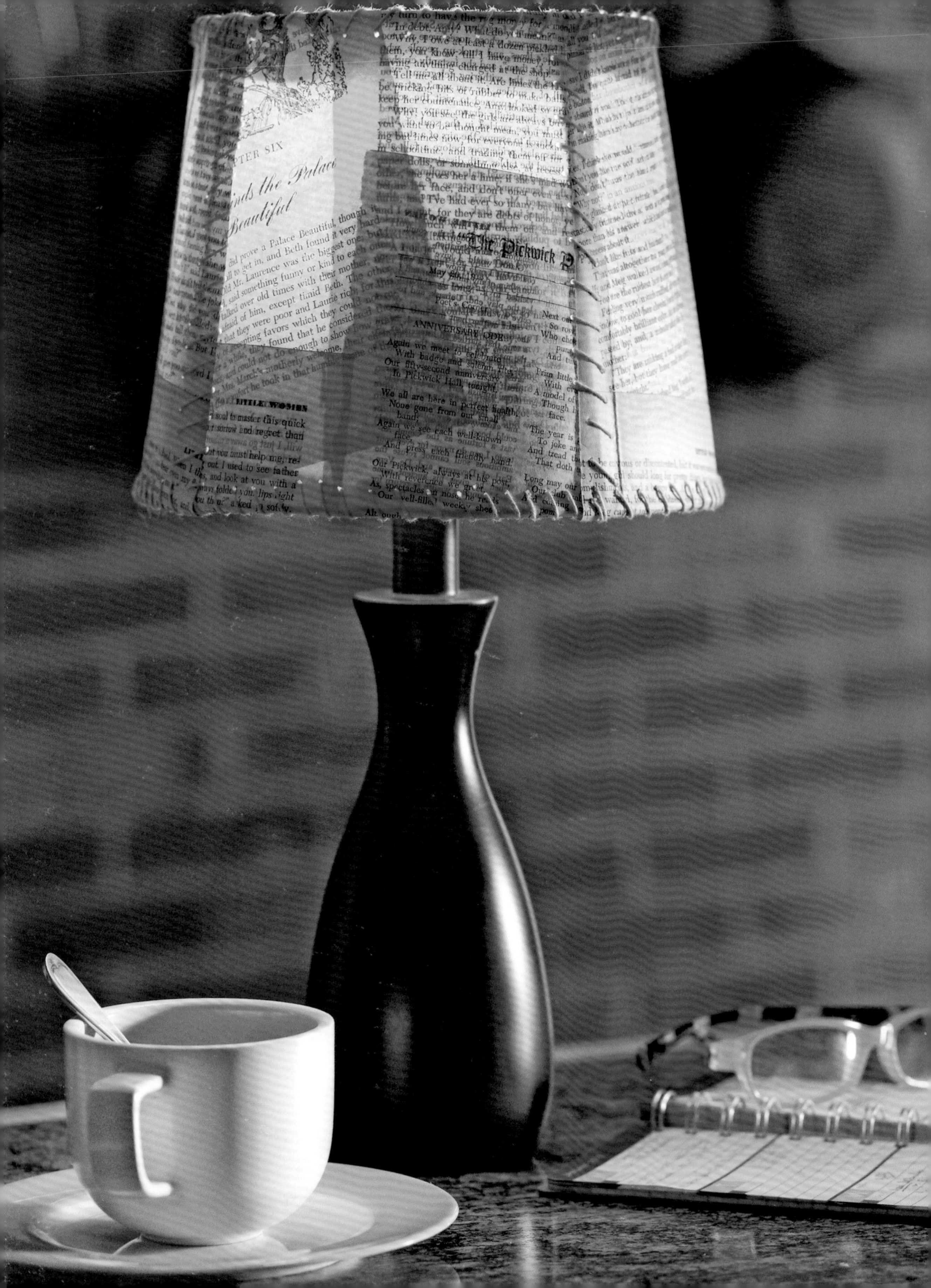
Beautiful
The Pickwick

LITERARY LAMPSHADE

by Charlotte Lyons

Charlotte Lyons is a designer, writer, and lifelong crafter. One day, she wrote a post on her blog, Wren Studio, about a lampshade she had constructed from old family letters. I couldn't help but think this would be a perfect way to utilize book pages—especially ones left over from projects that only repurpose a book cover. Charlotte graciously agreed to adapt her project for this book. As a decorative element, she also suggests stitching patterns and designs on the shade with a sewing machine.

Materials

Loose book pages, one or more pages for each lampshade panel

Boned lampshade (with metal rims and ribs), with or without fabric in any size or shape

Transparent vellum paper, enough to cover each lampshade panel

Yarn, twine, or cording

Tools

Craft knife

Metal ruler

Pencil

Scissors

Permanent marker

White glue and glue brush

Bone folder

Small office clamps

Sharp sewing needle with large eye

1. Select Pages for Lampshade

Choose pages from a book block left over from another project or from a fresh book. To remove pages, gently run your craft knife along the book's gutter, being careful to cut through only one page at a time.

2. Prepare Lampshade

If your lampshade came with fabric panels, cut off all the fabric with a craft knife.

3. Prepare Vellum

Measure the dimensions of each lampshade panel and draw the shape on transparent vellum, adding 2" to all sides. Cut out a piece of vellum for each panel in the shade. With permanent marker, number each panel on the lower rim of the lampshade frame. With a pencil, lightly number the corresponding vellum sheets.

4. Create Design

Select book pages to cover each vellum panel. Overlap the pages so that they cover the entire panel, making sure not to cover any text or illustrations you particularly like (Figure A). You can lay the pages out haphazardly (like the one shown here) or in a neater tiling pattern, if you prefer.

Sparingly brush glue onto the back of each book page and place on the vellum, smoothing it out with a bone folder. Note that the back side of the page will show through when the lamp is turned on, creating a double text pattern. Place all the glued panels under a stack of books and allow to dry thoroughly.

5. Trim Panels

Place each vellum/page panel on its corresponding shade panel, with the vellum on the inside; fold and press the edges along the metal ribs, leaving an impression. Retrace this line with a pencil immediately after pressing, then trace again, adding a ½" border to all lines. Trim each vellum/page panel along the outer traced line (Figure B).

6. Sew Panels

Center the first vellum/page panel over its corresponding panel on the lampshade. Use the small office clamps to attach the panel to the shade's ribs. Thread the sewing needle with a yard of yarn,

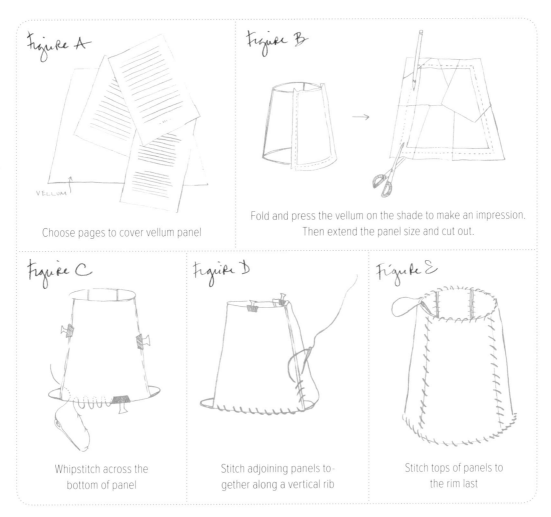

Figure A

Choose pages to cover vellum panel

Figure B

Fold and press the vellum on the shade to make an impression.
Then extend the panel size and cut out.

Figure C

Whipstitch across the
bottom of panel

Figure D

Stitch adjoining panels together along a vertical rib

Figure E

Stitch tops of panels to
the rim last

twine, or cording, and knot the end. Using a whipstitch, gently insert the needle on the bottom inside edge of the first panel. Carefully pull the needle through the vellum/page panel to the outside, exiting slightly above the rim. Then wrap the cording down around the rim and back to the inside, bringing the needle out ¼" from the first hole. Repeat this stitch along the bottom of the panel, keeping stitches spaced consistently and being careful not to tear the paper by pulling the stitches too tight (Figure C).

When you have attached the bottom of the first panel, center the second vellum/page panel over its corresponding section of the lampshade (the two vellum/page panels should overlap by ½"). Clamp the second panel to the ribs and whipstitch the two panels together along the vertical rib, encasing the rib in each stitch. To do this, insert the needle from the inside of the shade, about ¼" from the bottom edge, and then insert it about ¼" up on the other panel. Make sure the needle goes around the rib and reinsert it from the inside on the other panel, directly opposite the last stitch. Continue stitching this way up the length of the rib, keeping stitch lengths consistent (Figure D). Stitch the bottom of the second panel to its rim.

Continue securing each panel in this way until the bottoms and sides are attached. Then lace the tops of all panels to the top rim with one continuous line of whipstitches (Figure E). Trim and conceal all knots on the inside of the shade.

LOCKET BOOK

This nontraditional photo frame reminds me of a locket, since two photos are displayed facing each other. For the sample shown here, I used a copy of Dickens' *A Tale of Two Cities* and photos of each of my grandmothers when they were young women—they came from two different cities. At the moment, I don't intend to make any changes, but it's nice to know that I can easily slide out these photos and replace them with different ones if I want to.

Materials

Hardcover book, approximately 5" x 7"

2 photos, smaller than 4" x 5½"

9" x 12" piece black illustration board

Tools

Small office clips

White glue and glue brush

Clamps

Cutting mat

Metal ruler

Pencil

Craft knife

Masking tape

Cardboard scrap

Eraser

1. Glue Covers

Find the center of the book and open it to that page, laying the book flat. Count 25 pages to the left and clip these pages together with an office clip. Then count 25 pages to the right and clip these pages together. Flip all the pages to the left so that just the back cover is exposed. Brush glue on the inside back cover and close the cover, applying pressure to the book to secure the glue (Figure A). Flip all the pages to the right (so that just the front cover is exposed) and glue the front cover the same way.

2. Glue Book Block

Stand the book upright, with the pages set approximately at a 90-degree angle. Clamp each side of the book to hold the pages together tightly (keep the smaller clips on the 50 center pages). Generously brush glue onto the outer edges of the book block, starting at the top and working down the side (Figure B). Let the brush bristles sink into the crevices between the pages to make sure they fully adhere. Allow to dry completely, then turn the book upside down. Apply glue to the bottom of the book block, moving the clamps as necessary. Allow the book to dry completely. Note that gluing the book upright will help maintain its 90-degree angle.

3. Create Mat Board

Lay out the illustration board on a cutting mat. Measure and mark two 4" by 5½" rectangles, and cut out the pieces using a craft knife. Measure your photos and then subtract ¼" from the dimensions—this will be the size of the window in each illustration board. Draw the window shape on the center of both pieces of illustration board and cut it out with a craft knife. Place each photo in its window and secure the backside of the photo to the illustration board with two pieces of masking tape.

4. Cut Slots for Matted Photos

Open the book to its center point, with the 50 center pages evenly divided back into groups of 25 on each side. Center one matted photo on the left side of the loose book pages, tracing around the shape with a pencil. Then measure and mark ¼" in from all sides of this rectangle, creating a 3½" wide by 5" tall rectangle (the matted photo will sit behind this window). Place a piece of scrap cardboard under these 25 pages and, using a craft knife and ruler, cut through all 25 pages to make the window. Remove the scrap cardboard and trace this window on the glued block of pages beneath. Flip the loose pages back to the right and increase the width of the traced rectangle by ⅜" on each side, so that it is 4¼" wide. Draw lines extending the sides of the rectangle up to the top of the page (Figure C). Cut this shape from the glued book block, cutting about ⅛" deep (or deep enough to accommodate the matted photo). Repeat this step on the other side of the book. Then erase visible pencil lines from the center pages.

5. Glue Loose Pages and Insert Matted Photos

Open the book to its center point, with the loose pages to their respective sides. Remove the clips and clamp the pages to the rest of the book. Brush glue along the outer edges of the book block, concentrating on the loose pages, and allow to dry fully. Once dry, slip each photo into its slot and stand the book up to display (Figure D).

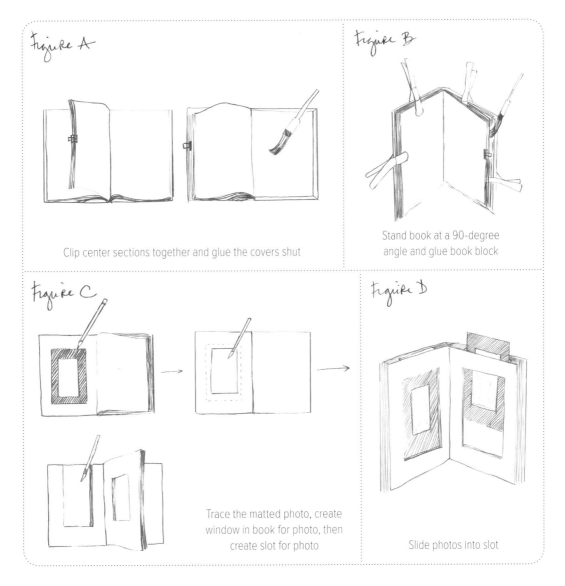

Figure A

Clip center sections together and glue the covers shut

Figure B

Stand book at a 90-degree angle and glue book block

Figure C

Trace the matted photo, create window in book for photo, then create slot for photo

Figure D

Slide photos into slot

PAGEWORK QUILT

This quilt is as an inexpensive and clever way to cover a naked wall—simply sew loose pages into a grid, then hang it up. Pages from just about any book will work, but for this project I chose illustrated pages from two different children's books. One book has black-and-white pencil drawings with text, while the other has colorful woodblock print illustrations. The "character" of the pages you choose will determine the overall feel of the finished quilt—and consequently, the room in which you might want to hang it. Note that older pages are more brittle and tear easily, so they are less suitable for this project.

Materials

25 loose book pages of approximately the same size (9 colorful/illustrated and 16 black-and-white/text only)
Note: My quilt is approximately 24" x 34", and is made from twenty-five 5½" x 7½" pages.

All-purpose thread, for sewing machine

Wood slatting, 1½" wide x 2" shorter than the width of the finished quilt

2 sawtooth hangers

Tools

Metal ruler

Pencil

Craft knife

Cutting mat

Masking tape

Sewing machine

Scissors

Superglue

Glue gun and glue sticks

1. Trim Pages and Lay Out Design

Before laying out the design, make sure that all 25 pages are the same size. Using your craft knife, ruler, and cutting mat, trim pages, if needed.

Once the pages are trimmed, lay them out in a 5 by 5 grid (as shown in the photo on page 119) to create an "X" pattern. (The colorful pages are used for the "X" portion of the design.)

2. Sew All Five Rows

Working with pages from the first row only, overlap the first two pages by ½" and temporarily secure the join with a small piece of masking tape. Tape the third and fourth pages together in the same way. With a sewing machine, sew the first two pages together with a straight stitch ¼" from the overlapped edge, carefully removing the masking tape as the needle approaches it. Sew the third page to the fourth page in the same way. Next, tape the second page to the third page and the fourth page to the fifth page, making sure that the overlaps are all going in the same direction. Sew those sheets together until you have joined all five pages in the first row (Figure A). Note that sewing through paper dulls the needle significantly, so only use this needle for paper projects going forward.

Repeat to construct the other four rows.

3. Join the Rows Together

Overlap rows 1 (the top row of your design) and 2 by ½" and use a few pieces of masking tape to temporarily secure the rows together. Using a sewing machine, sew the rows together, being very careful not to tear any of the edges. Make sure that you are sewing in the direction of the overlapped pages (not hitting the overlaps head on—see Figure B).

Repeat this process to attach each consecutive row. You may need to roll up the excess paper toward the last row so that it can fit through the machine—just make sure you don't fold the pages. Trim all loose threads.

4. Attach Slatting

Make sure the wood slatting is the proper length; it should be almost equal to the width of the stitched quilt. If it is wider, you'll need to cut it down to size. Center the two sawtooth hangers on the slatting about 1" from each end and glue in place with superglue (Figure C). Allow to dry completely.

Apply hot glue to the back of the slatting and attach it to the top of the quilt on its backside (Figure D). Give it a few minutes to set, and it's ready to hang!

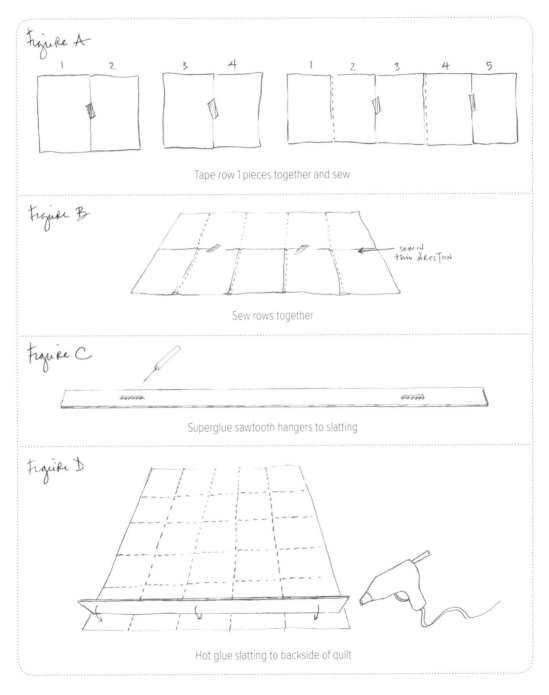

Figure A
Tape row 1 pieces together and sew

Figure B
sew in this direction
Sew rows together

Figure C
Superglue sawtooth hangers to slatting

Figure D
Hot glue slatting to backside of quilt

PLAYBOOK

A book safe is a classic repurposed book project. You know—it's where the smoking gun is hidden in movies, or perhaps the key to the safe-deposit box. My version is called a "playbook" since I used a book about bridge to store a deck of playing cards and a set of dice. To make a book safe, simply cut a hole in the book block big enough to store the object you have in mind. To that end, you'll need to make sure you use a book that is thick enough to hold the item. You can also turn the book into an art object by hot gluing items into the safe, like mementos from a trip, a seashell collection, or an array of vintage buttons.

Materials

Hardcover book

Decorative paper (optional)

Lightweight cardboard, for lining compartments

½ yard of ¼" ribbon (optional)

Tools

White glue and glue brush

Bone folder

Metal ruler

Pencil

Craft knife plus replacement blades

3 large clamps

Glue gun and glue sticks

1. Glue and Embellish Endpapers

Open the book to the back cover. Brush glue onto the inside back cover and press the next page to the cover, using the bone folder to smooth the paper.

Open the book to the front inside cover. If you would like to use decorative paper instead of the existing endpapers, measure and cut the paper to the same size as the existing endpapers. You'll need two pieces: one for the left endpaper (the inside front cover) and one for the right endpaper (the "first page" of the book safe). Brush glue on the backside of the decorative paper and press in place over the endpapers. Smooth the paper with a bone folder, making sure that it fits snugly in the crease at the gutter.

2. Glue Book Block

With the front cover open, secure the three outer edges of the book with clamps. Generously brush glue on all three sides of the book block, moving the clamps as needed. Let the brush bristles sink into the crevices between the pages to make sure they fully adhere. Keep the book clamped and let dry overnight.

3. Cut Compartments into Book Block

Measure the height (H), width (W), and depth (D) of the items you would like to store in your box to determine the shape of the holes you'll cut into the book block. For my "Playbook," I measured a deck of cards (2 ¼" W x 3 ½" H x ¾" D) and four dice lined up in a row (2 ½" W x ½" H x ½" D) in order to make two separate holes: one for the cards, and one for the dice. I then added ¼" on all sides of these two measurements for a little wiggle room.

When selecting where to place your holes, make sure to leave at least a 1" border of book block on all sides around the hole. With pencil and ruler, draw the dimensions of the holes on the first page of the book. Then run a craft knife along the perimeter of the holes using a ruler for accuracy (Figure A). I tend to cut through about 4 pages at a time, so reaching the desired depth (¾" for cards and ½" for the dice) can take a little time. As you cut, be sure that the corner edges meet at 90-degree angles, producing a nice clean edge. Change blades often to maintain clean cuts.

4. Line Compartment Walls

Once the desired hole depth has been reached, line its interior walls with lightweight cardboard to make it nice and neat. To do this, measure the height, width, and depth of each hole. Cut two pieces of cardboard to the dimensions of the W x D of each hole, and two pieces to the H x D of each hole (Figure B). Fit them inside the safe to be sure they fit, trimming if necessary.

If you wish, cover the cardboard with decorative paper or pages from the book. Consider the thickness of the papers to be sure that, when covered, the cardboard lining will still fit snugly into place. Trim, if necessary.

5. Attach Ribbon and Hole Lining

I added ribbons to my book safe so I could easily lift the deck of cards and dice from their niches. If you want to include ribbon, glue it in place before gluing the cardboard in place along the sides of the hole. To do this, cut a length of ribbon ⅓ longer than the length of the hole. Put a drop of hot glue on the inside edge of the hole and attach the end of the ribbon. Then apply hot glue to the backs of the cardboard pieces and glue in place along the hole's sides (Figure C).

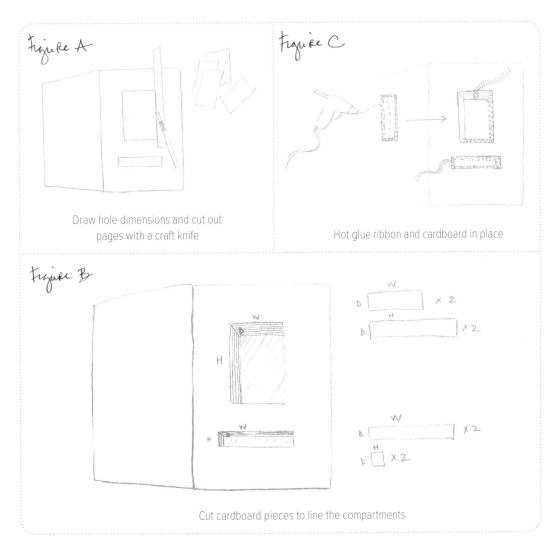

Draw hole dimensions and cut out pages with a craft knife

Hot glue ribbon and cardboard in place

Cut cardboard pieces to line the compartments

Pleated Sculpture

The beauty of this sculpture is in the simplicity of its creation—the pages are merely folded, with no cutting involved. The book's cover becomes the background of the piece, so the focus is on the printed pages which, when folded, take on a new three-dimensional form. The finished sculpture can either be hung on a wall or displayed on a flat surface.

Materials

Hardcover book, any size
   Note: The book should be in good condition with a sturdy, strong spine and nonbrittle pages.

Decorative paper, for recovering the endpapers (optional)

¼"-thick plywood, cut to 1" smaller than the dimensions of the book when it is opened flat (optional)

Tools

Metal ruler (optional)

Pencil (optional)

Craft knife (optional)

Cutting mat (optional)

White glue and glue brush (optional)

Bone folder

Drill and $5/32$" drill bit (optional)

Liquid Nails (optional)

4 clamps (optional)

2 nails (optional)

1. Cover Endpapers (optional)

Since the endpapers of the book will be on display, you may wish to cover them with decorative paper if you don't like the existing design on the book's endpapers. To do this, follow the instructions on page 15.

2. First Fold

Open the front cover of the book and begin folding in groups of two pages (including the loose endpaper in your first fold). Fold the lower right corner of the first two pages so that it meets the spine edge (Figure A). Crease with the bone folder.

3. Second Fold

Fold the upper right corner of the first two pages down to meet the spine and crease with a bone folder (Figure B). The two folds will overlap, forming a triangle with a point at the outer edge (Figure C).

4. Continue Folding

Repeat Steps 3 and 4 until all you have folded all of the pages in the book (Figure D). If your book has an odd number of pages, simply fold the last page by itself. If you wish to display the sculpture on a flat surface, you're done! If you want to hang it on a wall, you'll need to make a wall mount.

5. Create Wall Mount (Optional)

To make the holes for hanging, set the plywood on a work surface and mark two spots that are an equal distance from the top edge and either side (Figure E). Drill holes using a $5/32$" drill bit.

Apply Liquid Nails all over the surface of the wood, being careful not to drip in the drilled holes, and place the bottom side of the book sculpture on top. The book cover should hang over the edge of the wood on all sides. Clamp the top and bottom of the sculpture on both sides and allow to dry overnight (Figure F). Hammer nails into the wall to align with the drilled holes and hang the sculpture.

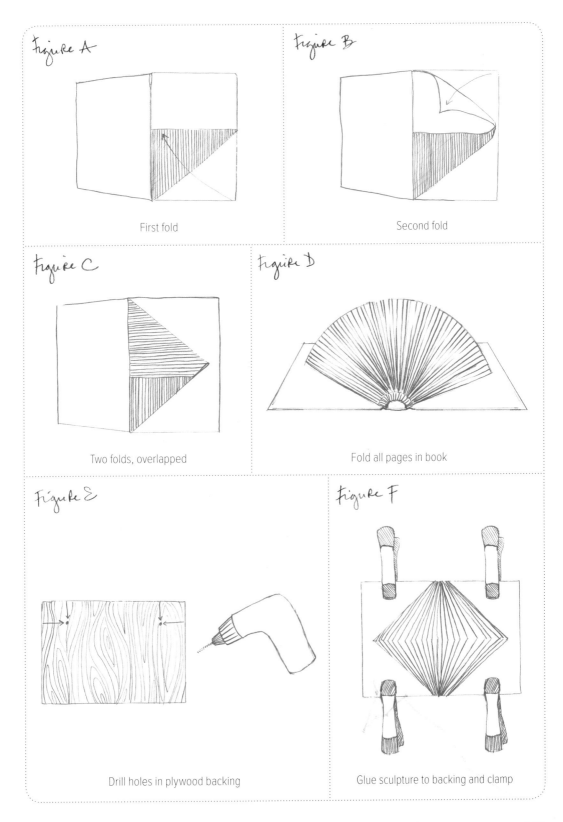

Figure A

First fold

Figure B

Second fold

Figure C

Two folds, overlapped

Figure D

Fold all pages in book

Figure E

Drill holes in plywood backing

Figure F

Glue sculpture to backing and clamp

Narrative Vases

A beautiful and unique art object, this vase gets its name more from the shape than from its functionality. Whether you make a single vase or create a grouping, the results are nothing less than enchanting. This is a perfect way to use up book blocks left over from other projects—just be sure the block has at least 150 pages. Book pages with type give the vase a great uniform look, but it can also be stunning to use pages from an illustrated book, such as one on flowers or trees, so that an occasional image peeks out from within the vase. I included several templates for vase shapes in these instructions, but I encourage you to sketch your own designs, too.

Materials

Book block from hardcover book or whole paperback (at least 150 pages)

Cardboard (not corrugated), approximately the height and width of the book block

Tools

Pencil

Scissors

Craft knife plus replacement blades

Small office clip

Gluestick

1. Make Vase Template

Place the book block or whole paperback on the cardboard, aligning it with the top left corner. Trace around the right and bottom sides of the book block with pencil.

Photocopy one of the vase templates at right, enlarging it to a size that fits within the dimensions of the book block. Cut out the shape from the photocopy and trace around it onto the cardboard (Figure A). Alternatively, you can draw a vase shape of your choosing onto the cardboard, leaving at least 1" of flat space for the base so that the vase will stand. Using a craft knife, cut out the vase shape from the cardboard.

2. Cut Shape from Book Block

Place the long, straight edge of the template along the spine of the book block. Hold very securely in place and carefully run the craft knife along the outer edge of the vase template, cutting through several pages at once (Figure B).

Continue cutting pages around the template, flipping over the cut pages and clamping them together with a small office clip as you work. Reposition the template over the uncut pages and continue cutting until all the pages have been cut (Figure C). To maintain accurate cuts, you may need to change the blade on the craft knife if the blade gets dull.

3. Finish Vase

When the cutting is complete, glue the first and last pages of the book together with gluestick (Figure D). Stand upright and enjoy!

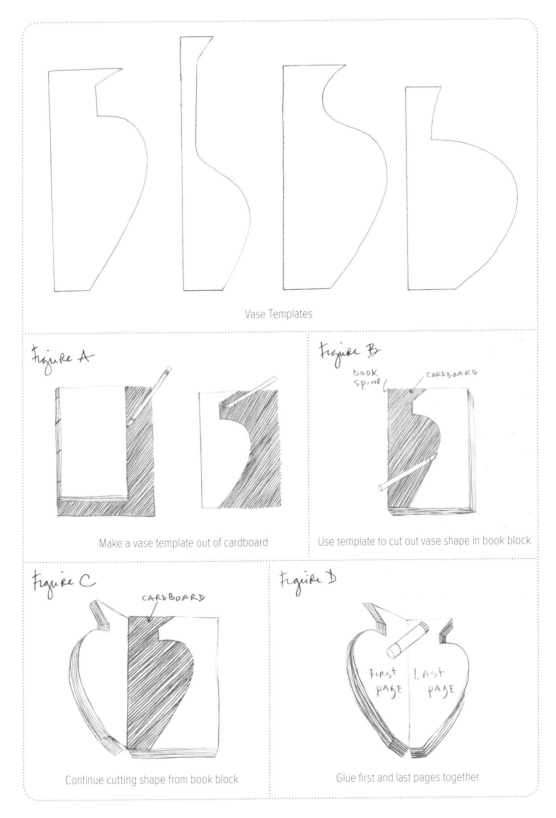

Vase Templates

Figure A

Make a vase template out of cardboard

Figure B

BOOK SPINE   CARDBOARD

Use template to cut out vase shape in book block

Figure C

CARDBOARD

Continue cutting shape from book block

Figure D

FIRST PAGE   LAST PAGE

Glue first and last pages together

ILLUMINATED SWITCH PLATE

This decoupaged switch plate is one of the simplest projects in this book, but it adds a touch of character to any room. All you need is a standard switch plate cover and an interesting page from a book—choose one with pretty type, an illustration, or a message you'd like to see as you're coming and going.

Materials

Switch plate cover and screws (for a single light switch)

Loose book page, at least ½" larger on all sides than the switch plate cover

Tools

Mod Podge

¼" glue brush

Cutting mat

Craft knife

Metal ruler

Awl

Screwdriver

1. Decoupage Switch Plate

Brush Mod Podge on the backside of the loose book page. Place the switch plate cover, front side down, on top of the book page (Figure A).

2. Trim the Page

Lay the switch plate cover and paper on a cutting mat. Using a craft knife and ruler, trim the edges of the paper so that it is ½" larger than the switch plate cover on all sides. Trim the corners of the paper on a diagonal, leaving about ¼" between the switch plate cover and the corner. Brush more Mod Podge on the edges of the paper, and then wrap the paper around the edges of the switch plate cover, pressing into place (Figure B). Turn the switch plate cover over and brush Mod Podge on the front side. Allow to dry completely.

3. Cut Hole for Light Switch

With the switch plate facedown on the cutting mat, cut an 'X' in the switch hole with a craft knife. Brush Mod Podge on the back of these triangles and fold them to the backside of the switch plate (Figure C).

4. Make Holes for Screws and Install

With the switch plate cover face up, use an awl to poke through the screw holes (Figure D). Then screw the switch plate cover over the light switch.

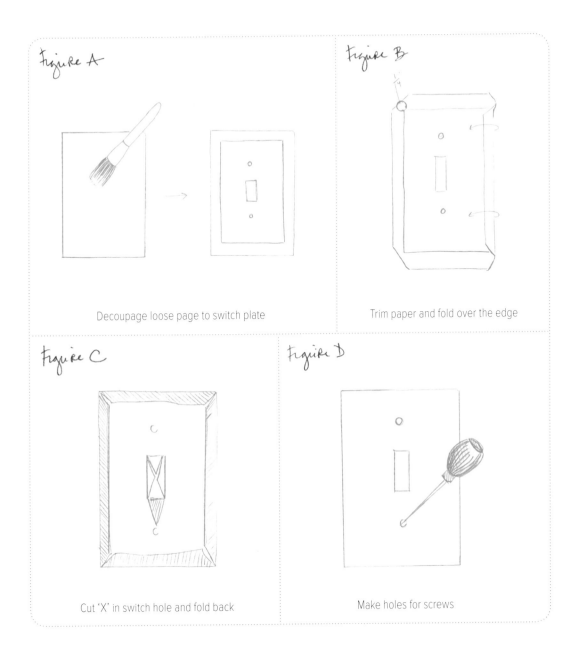

Figure A

Decoupage loose page to switch plate

Figure B

Trim paper and fold over the edge

Figure C

Cut 'X' in switch hole and fold back

Figure D

Make holes for screws

TOOL BIN

This project is both practical and easy—simply remove the book block from a hardcover book, enclose the open ends, and fill your new container with any utensils, tools, or implements you like. In this case I've transformed a book bin into a kitchen container to hold spoons, spatulas, and other cooking gadgets. A vintage cookbook was an obvious and charming choice.

Materials

Hardcover book, with spine at least 1½" wide

3" x 36" piece of ¼"-thick balsa wood

Decorative paper (optional)

Tools

Craft knife

Cutting mat

Pencil

Metal ruler

White glue and glue brush

Bone folder

Glue gun and glue sticks

1. Remove Book Block

Using a craft knife and following the instructions on page 13, remove the book block. Repair the book's spine, if necessary, following the instructions on page 14.

2. Cut Balsa Wood

Measure and write down the book block's width, length, and depth. Lay the balsa wood on a cutting mat. With the ruler and craft knife, cut three pieces of balsa at the following measurements (Figure A):

> One bottom panel the depth and width of book block

> Two side panels the depth and length of book block

3. Cover Balsa Pieces

The balsa wood pieces will be covered with loose pages from the book block (or decorative paper, if you prefer). If using loose book pages you may need two sheets to fully cover the boards. Lay the book pages down on a cutting mat and place the cut balsa pieces over the paper. Trace around the balsa pieces onto the paper, leaving an extra ½" on all sides, then cut out the paper using a ruler and craft knife. Sparingly brush glue onto the wrong side of the paper. Center each piece of balsa on its corresponding paper piece and firmly press down. Flip the balsa over and smooth the paper with a bone folder. Turn over again and snip the corners of each piece of paper leaving a ¼" margin. Brush glue onto the edges of the paper and snugly fold it over the boards, pressing down to adhere (Figure B).

4. Glue Balsa in Place

Heat up the hot glue gun. Open the book cover so it's lying flat with the inside of the book facing up. Apply hot glue to the long edge of one balsa side panel and press to the inside spine. Then run hot glue along the long edge of the bottom panel and set into place at the bottom edge of the book, making sure it meets the book cover at a 90-degree angle. Hold the bottom piece in place for at least 20 seconds to let the glue set. Attach the other side panel to the side of the book as you did for the bottom panel, making sure that the side panel and bottom panel meet at a 90-degree angle. Then run a little hot glue along the inside edge where the two pieces meet to secure the join (Figure C).

5. Glue Book Bin Shut

Run hot glue along the top edges of the side and bottom panels and along the short exposed edge of the bottom panel (Figure D). Quickly close the front cover of the book and hold in place for at least 20 seconds to let the glue set.

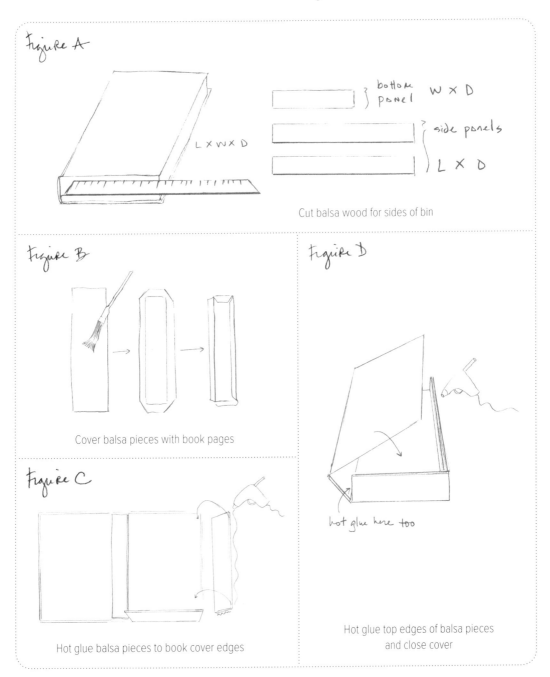

Figure A

L X W X D

bottom panel   W X D

side panels   L X D

Cut balsa wood for sides of bin

Figure B

Cover balsa pieces with book pages

Figure D

hot glue here too

Hot glue top edges of balsa pieces and close cover

Figure C

Hot glue balsa pieces to book cover edges

RESOURCES

FINDING BOOKS LOCALLY

Some of the best places to find books to repurpose are right in your own community. Check out thrift shops, yard sales, recycling centers, antique shops, flea markets, library sales, and even your own attic and bookshelves.

Librarians and used bookstore owners are particularly great resources for locating specific books, since they typically have overflowing storage rooms. Old nonfiction books from libraries, such as textbooks and almanacs, are perfect to use since their information is outdated and they have lots of photographs and illustrations. By helping libraries and used bookstores clear out space, you're doing them a favor, so in some cases they might be willing to give you a sweet deal. Also, check with your local bookstores and libraries to see if they ever hold charity book sales.

FINDING BOOKS ON THE INTERNET

The Internet can be a great source for locating used books, especially if you are seeking something specific (and at a particular price). Here is a quick reference list of several helpful websites.

bookfinder.com A site solely devoted to the sale of new, used, and rare books—it searches more than 100 different sellers for titles.

booksalefinder.com Covering the U.S. and Canada, this site lists book sales, auctions, and book fairs in the area you select.

craigslist.org An online "classified" section, divided into myriad categories and sorted by city and state. Look under "books" or "free" listings, or place a "want ad" for specific books.

earth911.com A way to find places in your community to procure, donate, or dispose of any materials (like books).

ebay.com A shopping and auction site for nearly anything, but especially helpful if you are looking for a specific book genre or title and need to refine your search.

gotbooks.com An organization that promotes the re-selling (and donation) of books for profit and nonprofit programs.

librarybooksales.org A way to purchase books online from libraries across the U.S. Proceeds go directly to the library from which you purchased the books.

recyclingcenters.org Listings for local recycling centers.

swaptree.com A way to trade books with users all over the world.

SOURCES FOR SUPPLIES

Most of the materials and tools for the projects in this book can be found at art supply and hardware stores. For specific materials, try these online sources.

Music Box Element (for Music Book, page 103)
www. kikkerland.com/prod/1201.htm

Light Cord Set (for Three-Book Chandelier, page 72)
www.ikea.com

Library Pocket (for Kindle Keeper, page 85)
www.gaylord.com

CREDITS

Accessories and bric-a-brac provided by Urban Outfitters. Paintings on pages 46 and 48 by Grace Fontaine.